Educational
Rights
of Children
with
Disabilities

Educational Rights of Children with Disabilities

▼

A Primer for Advocates

**Eileen L. Ordover
and Kathleen B. Boundy**

Center for Law and Education
Cambridge, Massachusetts

A copy of this book has been sent to every main and branch office of programs funded by the Legal Services Corporation. Replacement copies are available. For ordering information contact the Center for Law and Education, 955 Massachusetts Avenue, Cambridge, MA 02139, (617) 876-6611.

Funds for the preparation of this book were provided by the Legal Services Corporation and the Agent Orange Class Assistance Program (through a sub-contract with the Mental Health Law Project). The opinions expressed are those of the authors. This publication cannot substitute for the independent judgment of a competent attorney or other professional.

Editor: Sharon Schumack
Cover design: Mia Saunders

ISBN 0-912585-06-4

Contents

About This Book

Educational Rights of Children with Disabilities: A Primer for Advocates analyzes rights under two federal statutes, the Individuals with Disabilities Education Act (IDEA)* and Section 504 of the Rehabilitation Act of 1973.

These statutes were enacted in the early 1970's to combat pervasive discrimination against people with disabilities. IDEA, §504 and their respective implementing regulations provide comprehensive and detailed educational rights to children with disabilities. They are not, however, the only sources of students' rights and protections. The educational rights of children with disabilities are also shaped by their constitutional rights to equal protection of the laws and due process, civil rights statutes prohibiting discrimination on the basis of race and sex, federal statutes providing equal educational opportunity to limited English proficient students, certain basic guarantees to homeless students, and quality programming to youth in vocational education and to educationally disadvantaged students participating in compensatory education programs.

This book must also be read together with your state's statutes, regulations and judicial decisions regarding the educational rights of children who have disabilities. IDEA and §504 establish both entitlements and prohibitions against certain kinds of state and local practices. State law, however, may provide students with disabilities additional rights and protections. At a minimum, state law provides the details for IDEA and §504 implementation and compliance. If state law undermines, contradicts or violates IDEA or §504 mandates, it is, of course, invalid.

Legal research for this book was completed in July, 1991, and it went to press in September, 1991. The administrative materials and judicial decisions cited for various points are intended, by and

---

* This law, formerly entitled the Education of the Handicapped Act (EHA), encompasses several pieces of legislation, including the Education for All Handicapped Children Act, P. L. 94-142.

large, to be illustrative rather than comprehensive. Advocates should thus be aware of the need to research further the law in their respective jurisdictions, in addition to updating our research as needed.

A note about language: As our title suggests, we choose the terms "disability" and "children with disabilities" over "handicap" or "children with handicaps" or "handicapped children." Prior to 1990, IDEA was entitled the Education of the Handicapped Act, and used "handicap" and its permutations throughout. As of this writing, the regulations implementing IDEA still use "handicap" in its various forms (although changes have been proposed), as do §504, the §504 regulations, and many of the judicial decisions discussed in this book. Where we have deemed it important to track the language of a particular statute, regulation or decision, we, too, have used such terminology.

Attorneys and legal workers will be familiar with the legal notations, symbols and citations used, particularly in the endnotes. Others may find their meaning less than obvious. Appendix A explains the general format for citing cases, statutes and regulations and includes an explanation of the various symbols, notations and abbreviations used in this book. Appendix B contains the addresses and telephone numbers of the regional offices of the U.S. Department of Education's Office for Civil Rights, which are responsible for investigating complaints alleging violations of §504.

I.
The Federal Statutory Framework:
The Individuals with Disabilities Education Act and Section 504 of the Rehabilitation Act of 1973

A. The Individuals With Disabilities Education Act or "IDEA"

Congress enacted P.L. 94-142, the Education for All Handicapped Children Act[1] in 1975 in response to the widespread failure of public school systems to provide appropriate — or in many cases, any — education to children with disabilities. The Act, which was renamed the Individuals With Disabilities Education Act ("IDEA") in 1990, provides states with funds for special education programs. In return, a state accepting these funds — as well as the local school systems to which it channels them — must comply with the substantive and procedural requirements set forth in IDEA. All fifty states accept IDEA funds.

IDEA requires states and local education agencies to provide a "free appropriate public education" for all "children with disabilities."[2] The statute and the U.S. Department of Education regulations implementing it set forth requirements for identifying and evaluating "children with disabilities," the components of a free appropriate public education, the process by which such an education is to be designed for individual children, and the procedures by which their parents and guardians may challenge the adequacy of the education offered them.

The Office of Special Education Programs or "OSEP," a division of the U.S. Department of Education, is responsible for administering and enforcing IDEA. In addition, state departments of education are responsible for ensuring that local school districts (as well as other public, and in certain instances, private, agencies in the state that provide educational services) comply with IDEA. The Act is also enforced through administrative and judicial actions initiated by parents and students who allege that their IDEA rights have been violated.

1. Eligibility

Only those students who are "children with disabilities" within the meaning of IDEA are entitled to its protections. For purposes of IDEA,

> "[t]he term 'children with disabilities' means children...with mental retardation, hearing impairments including deafness, speech or language impairments, visual impairments including blindness, serious emotional disturbance, orthopedic impairments, autism, traumatic brain injury, other health impairments, or specific learning disabilities...who *by reason thereof need special education and related services.*"[3]

The regulations implementing IDEA define each of these conditions in detail.[4]

Children whose disabilities come within these definitions are protected by IDEA and are eligible for the education it guarantees regardless of the severity of their disabilities.[5] *IDEA does not allow for the possibility that some children are too severely disabled to be served; states and school systems may not refuse to provide educational services on the ground that a child is too severely disabled to benefit from them.*[6]

2. Age Ranges

IDEA compels states to serve all children with disabilities aged three through twenty-one years *unless*, with respect to 3 through 5 year olds and 18 through 21 year olds, this requirement would be inconsistent with a state law or practice or a court order.[7] If a state, school district or other public agency does undertake to serve 3 through 5 or 18 through 21 year olds, however, all of IDEA's substantive and procedural requirements apply.[8]

Amendments to IDEA have strengthened the financial incentive for states to serve three through five year olds by gradually increasing the federal funding available to states to serve this group.[9] Beginning with the 1991-92 school year, participating states must serve *all* three through five year olds with disabilities within their jurisdictions, or lose federal funding for services for this age group.[10]

B. Section 504 of the Rehabilitation Act of 1973

Section 504 of the Rehabilitation Act of 1973 is a civil rights statute designed to prohibit discrimination on the basis of disability. Modelled after Title VI of the Civil Rights Act of 1964 and Title IX of the Education Amendments of 1972 — which address racial or national origin and sex discrimination, respectively — it applies to recipients of federal funds. Section 504 as amended[11] provides in relevant part that:

"No otherwise qualified individual with handicaps in the United States...shall, solely by reason of his handicap, be excluded from participation in, be denied the benefit of, or be subject to discrimination under any program or activity receiving federal financial assistance..."[12]

Because virtually all local schools and school districts receive federal funds of some sort, §504 provides an additional tool for assuring that school-age children with disabilities receive the education to which they are entitled. Section 504 is enforced through administrative complaints and compliance reviews by the U.S. Department of Education's Office of Civil Rights or "OCR," and also through litigation by individuals who allege deprivation of their §504 entitlements.

1. Individuals Protected

For purposes of §504, an "individual with handicaps" is an individual who

"..(i) has a physical or mental impairment which substantially limits one or more major life activities, (ii) has a record of such an impairment, or (iii) is regarded as having such an impairment."[13]

"Major life activities" means activities such as caring for one's self, performing manual tasks, walking, seeing, hearing, speaking, breathing, learning and working.[14] Virtually all children eligible for special education and related services under IDEA will fall within this definition, and be protected by §504, as well.

The §504 definition of an "individual with handicaps," however, is broader than the IDEA definition of "children with disabilities," protecting many children who are *not* IDEA-eligible. For example, a child who has an "other health impairment," such as epilepsy or AIDS, for example, but who does not need specialized instruction and so is not a "child with disabilities" within the IDEA definition is nonetheless protected against discrimination by §504 and its implementing regulations. Similarly, a child who does not have any of the kinds of disabilities required for IDEA eligibility might nonetheless have an impairment — or be regarded as having an impairment or have a history of an impairment — covered by §504.[15]

In order to be protected from discrimination by §504, an "individual with handicaps" must be "otherwise qualified." For purposes of public preschool, elementary or secondary school services and activities, a child or student is "otherwise qualified" if she or he is:

- of an age during which non-handicapped individuals are provided with such services, or
- of any age during which it is mandatory under state law to provide such services to handicapped individuals, or
- is someone IDEA requires the state to provide with a free appropriate public education.[16]

2. Operation and Reach of §504

Regulations promulgated by the U.S. Department of Education interpret and implement §504's broad ban on discrimination as it applies to recipients of Department of Education funds.[17] In regard to preschool, elementary and secondary education, these regulations operate in two basic ways: by generally prohibiting certain practices as illegal, discriminatory ones and by compelling school systems to take certain affirmative steps to ensure that all students with disabilities receive a free appropriate public education.

Free Appropriate Public Education Like IDEA, the regulations implementing §504 require public school systems to provide a free appropriate public education in the least restrictive environment regardless of the nature or severity of a student's disability.[18] Unlike IDEA, a free appropriate public education under §504 may include "regular" education as well as "special" education.[19] Many specific §504 requirements concerning issues such as the evaluation and placement of pupils with disabilities, the components of a free appropriate education, the circumstances under which a student with disabilities may be removed from the regular education setting, and procedural safeguards mirror or complement IDEA mandates.

Section 504 also protects students who attend private preschool, day care, elementary and secondary schools from disability-based discrimination *if* the school is a "program or activity receiving federal financial assistance."[20] The §504 obligations of such programs vary depending upon the kinds of programs and services they offer.[21]

Prohibited Discriminatory Practices   In addition to imposing specific requirements upon preschool, elementary and secondary school programs, the §504 regulations ban all recipients of Department of Education funds from engaging in certain discriminatory practices. Key illegal practices include:

- denying a "qualified handicapped person" the opportunity to participate in or benefit from an aid, benefit or service;[22]
- affording a "qualified handicapped person" an opportunity to participate in or benefit from an aid, benefit or service that is not equal to that afforded others;[23]
- providing a "qualified handicapped person" with an aid, benefit or service that is not as effective as that provided to others;[24]
- providing different or separate aid, benefits or services to "handicapped persons" or to any class of "handicapped persons" unless such action is necessary to provide "qualified handicapped persons" with aid, benefits, or services that are as effective as those provided to others;[25]
- denying a "qualified handicapped person" the benefits of any program or activity, excluding him or her from participation, or otherwise subjecting him or her to discrimination because a recipient's facilities are inaccessible to or unusable by people with disabilities;[26]
- otherwise limiting a "qualified handicapped person" in the enjoyment of any right, privilege, advantage, or opportunity enjoyed by others receiving an aid, benefit or service.[27]

These broad prohibitions have been used successfully to challenge a wide variety of school system practices not specifically addressed by other §504 regulations or IDEA.[28] Although the following chapters focus chiefly on specific, affirmative requirements under §504 and IDEA, advocates should keep these general prohibitions in mind as well in asserting and defending educational rights.

Notes

1. 20 U.S.C. §1400 et seq. Prior to 1990 the Act, as amended, was referred to as the Education of the Handicapped Act (EHA).

2. 20 U.S.C. §§1412(1) and 1414(a).

3. 20 U.S.C. §1401(a)(1) (emphasis added).

4. See 34 C.F.R. §300.5(b). "Autism" and "traumatic brain injury," which were added to IDEA by the Education of the Handicapped Act Amendments of 1990, Pub. L. 101-476, 104 Stat. 1103, were not yet defined by regulation at the time of this writing. Apart from the 1990 addition of autism as a categorical disability, "autistic condition" is included and defined by regulation as a subcategory of "other health impaired." See 34 C.F.R. §300.5(b). The Department of Education published proposed regulations defining "autism" and "traumatic brain injury" (and eliminating "autistic condition" as a subcategory of "other health impaired") on August 19, 1991. See 56 Fed. Reg. 41271 (1991).

Earlier versions of what became Pub. L. 101-476 would have also added Attention Deficit Disorder ("ADD") as a categorical disability triggering IDEA eligibility. The final legislation instead directed the Department of Education to publish a notice in the Federal Register seeking public comment on eight issues pertaining to the definition of ADD and its inclusion in IDEA. See §102 of Pub. L. 101-476, 104 Stat. at 1105. Responses were to be summarized and forwarded to the Senate Committee on Labor and Human Resources and the House Committee on Education and Labor. *Id.* As of August 1991, Congress had not taken further action on the matter.

5. 20 U.S.C. §§1412(2)(C) and 1414(a)(1)(A).

6. Timothy W. v. Rochester School District, 875 F.2d 954 (1st Cir. 1989), *cert. denied*, 110 S. Ct. 519.

7. 20 U.S.C. §1412(2)(B); 34 C.F.R. §300.300.

8. 34 C.F.R. §300.300(b)(4).

9. See Title II of Pub. L. 99-457, codified at 20 U.S.C. §1419.

10. *Id.*

11. 29 U.S.C. §794.

12. 29 U.S.C. §794(a).

13. 29 U.S.C. §706(8)(B).

14. 34 C.F.R. §104.3(j)(2)(ii). The term "physical or mental impairment" means any physiological disorder or condition, cosmetic disfigurement, or anatomical loss affecting one or more of the neurological, musculoskeletal, sense organs, respiratory (including speech organs), cardiovascular, reproductive, digestive, genito-urinary, hemic and lymphatic, skin or endocrine systems, as well as any mental or psychological disorder, such as mental retardation, organic brain syndrome, emotional or mental illness, and specific learning disabilities. 34 C.F.R. §104.3(j)(2)(i).

15. For example, a student who has been erroneously classified as having mental retardation or who has a record of "incorrigible" behavior might be "regarded as having...an impairment" or have "a record of...an impairment" for purposes of §504. In addition, a child who does not have any of the disabilities listed in IDEA might nonetheless have an actual, current "impairment" for §504 purposes. A child who is HIV positive but asymptomatic — and so not "other health impaired" as defined by IDEA — would fall within this category. See Chapter VII, *infra*.

16. 34 C.F.R. §104.3(k)(2).

17. The Department's §504 regulations are codified at 34 C.F.R. part 104.

18. 34 C.F.R. §§104.33(a), 104.34(a).

19. 34 C.F.R. §104.33(b).

20. 29 U.S.C. §794(a). For the definition of "program or activity," see 29 U.S.C. §794(b). Private schools that do *not* receive federal financial assistance may be "public accommodations" subject to the anti-discrimination provisions of Title III of the Americans with Disabilities Act of 1990. *See* Pub. L. 101-336, §301(7)(J), 104 Stat. 327, 354, to be codified at 42 U.S.C. §12181.

21. Preschool and day care programs and activities may not exclude qualified children with disabilities on the basis of disability, and must take their needs into account in determining the aid, benefits or services to be provided by the program or activity. 34 C.F.R. §104.38. Private elementary and secondary programs may not exclude a qualified student with disabilities "if the person can, with minor adjustments, be provided an appropriate education..." 34 C.F.R. §104.39(a). Private elementary and secondary schools that operate special education programs must abide by §504 requirements regarding evaluation and placement, procedural safeguards, least restrictive environment, non-academic services, and comparability of facilities and services identifiable as serving students with disabilities to other facilities and services operated by the recipient. 34 C.F.R. §104.39(c). The §504 regulations also limit the extent to which private elementary and secondary schools may impose excess charges for services to students with disabilities. *See* 34 C.F.R. §104.39(b).

In addition, all private preschools, day care programs and elementary and secondary school programs that are recipients of federal funds must comply with the "General Provisions" and "Program Accessibility" subparts of the Department of Education's §504 regulations, appearing at 34 C.F.R. §§104.1 *et seq.* and §§104.21 *et seq.*, respectively (as must public school systems). Among the issues addressed by these two subparts are architectural accessibility and particular prohibited discriminatory practices.

22. 34 C.F.R. §104.4(b)(1)(i).

23. 34 C.F.R. §104.4(b)(1)(ii).

24. 34 C.F.R. §104.4(b)(1)(iii).

25. 34 C.F.R. §104.4(b)(1)(iv).

26. 34 C.F.R. §104.21. This provision should be read along with 34 C.F.R. §§104.22, 104.23, which delineate the circumstances under which recipients need or need not remove architectural barriers in order to meet this requirement.

27. 34 C.F.R. §104.4(b)(1)(vii).

28. See, for example, Garaway (OH) Local School District, 17 EHLR [Education of the Handicapped Law Report] 237 (OCR 9/13/90) (carrying mobility impaired student on and off school bus rather than providing accessible transportation); Sumter County (SC) School District #17, 17 EHLR 193 (OCR 9/28/90) (disabled student disciplined more harshly than others); Duchesne County (UT) School District, 17 EHLR 240 (OCR 9/13/90) (providing special education students with shorter school day and longer bus rides than regular education students); New Carlisle-Bethel Local School District, EHLR 257:477 (OCR 1/30/84) (inaccessible classrooms prevented mobility impaired student from taking certain classes); Tucson (AZ) Unified School District No. 1, EHLR 352:47 (OCR 2/16/84) (failure to utilize adaptive equipment in order to make driver's education course accessible to mobility impaired students); Fayette County (KY) School District, EHLR 353:279 (OCR 3/1/89) (admission to after school program); Jefferson County (KY) School District, EHLR 353:176 (OCR 9/19/88) (admission to summer enrichment program); Carbon-Lehigh (PA) Intermediate School District #21, EHLR 352:108 (OCR 9/20/85) (offering only limited electives in segregated school for emotionally disturbed students in comparison to range of electives available to regular education students).

II.
Content, Quality and the Meaning of "Free Appropriate Public Education"

IDEA requires school systems to provide eligible children with a "free appropriate public education" consisting of "special education and related services."[1] For purposes of §504, a "free appropriate public education" may consist of either "special education" or "regular education" and "related aids and services."[2] Both statutes also call for a child with disabilities to be educated in regular education settings with non-disabled peers to the maximum extent appropriate in view of his or her individual needs.[3] This latter requirement is often referred to as "least restrictive environment" or "mainstreaming."

Another component of the "free appropriate public education" mandated by IDEA is the Individualized Education Program or "IEP" that school systems must design at least annually for each child with disabilities. Under IDEA, a school system is *not* providing a free appropriate public education if it is not following a properly developed IEP.[4]

An IEP must, among other things, set forth annual goals and instructional objectives for the student, describe the special education and related services the child is to receive, and specify the extent to which he or she will be integrated with non-disabled peers.[5] School systems have an affirmative obligation to keep abreast of promising new methods and strategies for meeting the educational needs of children with disabilities, and to employ them as appropriate in designing and implementing IEPs.[6]

IDEA and its regulations set forth extensive requirements governing the process through which these determinations are to be made and the IEP developed. These requirements, along with those governing the content of IEPs, are discussed below in Chapter V. Requirements governing the educational evaluations upon which IEPs must be based are discussed in Chapter IV.

Section 504 does not require the development of an IEP. However, the §504 regulations provide that implementation of an IEP developed pursuant to IDEA is one means of providing an "appropriate" education under §504.[7]

A. The Meaning of "Appropriate": Procedural Compliance, Educational Quality, and the Concept of "Benefit"

1. IDEA

IDEA defines "free appropriate public education" by simply describing its components: special education and related services meeting state and IDEA standards provided at public expense, with no cost to parent or child, under public supervision, in conformity with the child's IEP.[8] A "free appropriate public education" must also "...meet the standards of the State educational agency...[and] include an appropriate preschool, elementary or secondary education in the State involved..."[9] Nowhere, however, does IDEA actually define the term "appropriate." Put another way, neither IDEA nor its regulations specify how well a package of special education and related services must meet a child's needs in order to be deemed "appropriate."

The U.S. Supreme Court took up this issue in *Board of Education of the Hendrick Hudson Central School District v. Rowley.*[10] In *Rowley*, the court ruled that the special education and related services offered a child with disabilities must meet two criteria in order to be "appropriate" for purposes of IDEA:

> (1) the IEP must be developed in accordance with the procedures set forth in IDEA, including those governing resolution of disputes between parents and school systems
>
> AND
>
> (2) the IEP must be "reasonably calculated to enable the child to receive educational benefits."[11]

The requirement that an IEP enable a student to receive educational benefits in order to be deemed "appropriate" does *not* mean that *any* degree of benefit is enough to satisfy IDEA standards. "*De minimis*" or trivial benefit is not enough; *rather, the IEP must be one "under which educational **progress** is likely."*[12]

In developing this two-part test for "appropriateness," *Rowley* held that IDEA does not require states and school systems to provide education designed to maximize the potential of children with disabilities.[13] Advocates, however, should pay close attention to their *state's* law concerning the quality of education to which children with disabilities are entitled. As interpreted in *Rowley*, IDEA sets a "basic floor" for special education quality. It does *not* prohibit states from setting higher quality and benefit standards,[14] and a number of states do so by statute, regulation, judicial decision, or state constitutional provision.[15] Because special education and related services must meet the standards of the state educational agency,[16] where a higher state quality standard exists, it is automatically "incorporated" into IDEA.[17] *In these states an education meeting the higher state quality standard is an IDEA right, and IDEA compliance may thus require IEPs designed to maximize potential or otherwise exceed the Rowley benefit standard.*

On an issue related to educational quality, school districts must insure that the variety of educational programs and services available to children in the system who do not have disabilities — such as art, music, industrial arts, consumer and homemaking education and vocational education — is available to children with disabilities as well.[18] This requirement encompasses all programs and services in which children without disabilities participate,[19] and applies to all children with disabilities, regardless of the school or educational program they attend. School systems must also make physical education services available to all children with disabilities, specially designing it to meet individual needs if necessary.[20]

2. §504

Unlike IDEA, §504 does provide a standard for determining whether the education provided a child with disabilities is "appropriate" and otherwise substantively sufficient. Section 504 regulations actually provide two such measures.

Appropriateness First, for purposes of §504, "appropriate education" means regular or special education and related aids and services "designed to meet the individual educational needs of handicapped persons as adequately as the needs of nonhandicapped persons are met."[21] Implementation of an IEP developed in the manner set forth in IDEA is one way of meeting this requirement.[22] In order to be "appropriate" within the meaning of §504 education must also be based upon adherence to §504 requirements governing placement in the least restrictive environment, evaluations and procedural safeguards for students and parents (including notice and hearing rights and access to student records).[23] These requirements are discussed below in Chapters II(D), IV and VI, respectively.

Comparable Benefits and Services   Section 504 also requires school systems to provide students with disabilities with benefits and services comparable to those provided to non-disabled students.   This requirement flows from regulations prohibiting the following, among others, as "discriminatory practices":

- affording a disabled student an opportunity to participate in or benefit from an aid, a benefit or a service that is not equal to that afforded others; and
- providing a disabled student with an aid, benefit or service that is not as effective as that provided to others.[24]

Advocates may use these regulations to challenge a wide variety of discriminatory practices.   These regulations make it illegal, for example, for a school district to provide children with disabilities with a shorter school day than that provided non-disabled students, except when a shorter day is "demonstrably required by the individual educational needs" of a particular child.[25]

In addition, the regulations expressly provide that any facility that is identifiable as being for students with disabilities must be comparable, in terms of both the facility itself and the services and activities conducted in it, to facilities for non-disabled students.[26]

B. The Meaning of "Special Education"

As used in IDEA, "special education" does not refer to any particular classroom, school or other setting in which children with disabilities are educated. "Special education" merely means "*specially designed* instruction...to meet the *unique* needs of a child with disabilities."[27]   Once instruction for an individual child has been so tailored to address his or her needs it may, again depending upon the child's needs, be provided in a variety of settings including a regular education classroom. Thus a school district cannot fulfill its obligation to provide "special education" by, for example, automatically placing a child with a particular disability in a particular classroom or program designated to serve that group.[28]   In addition to circumventing IDEA requirements, such conduct constitutes illegal discrimination under §504.[29]

C. The Meaning and Scope of "Related Services"

The related services mandated by IDEA consist of "[t]ransportation and such developmental, corrective and other supportive services...as may be required *to assist a child with disabilities to benefit from special education.*"[30] Under both IDEA and §504, the particular related services a child is to receive must be based upon an individualized determination of his or her unique needs — *not* upon the category of his or her disability.[31] Thus, for example, a rule or policy that allowed only children with severe emotional disturbance to receive counseling as a related service would violate both statutes.

1. Transportation

Where needed to accommodate the needs of a child receiving special education under IDEA, transportation includes:

- travel to and from school and between schools where a student's educational program is provided at more than one site;
- travel in and around school buildings; and
- specialized equipment such as special or adapted buses, lifts and ramps.[32]

2. Developmental, Corrective and Supportive Services

IDEA and its regulations list the following as *examples* of developmental, corrective and supportive services falling within the category of "related services":

- speech pathology and audiology;
- psychological services;
- physical therapy;
- occupational therapy;
- medical services for diagnostic or evaluation purposes, provided by a licensed physician to determine a child's medically related disability resulting in a need for special education and related services;
- recreation, including assessment of leisure function, therapeutic recreation services, leisure education and recreation programs in schools and community agencies;
- counseling services provided by social workers, psychologists,

    guidance counselors or other qualified personnel;
- parent training and counseling aimed at assisting parents in understanding the needs of their child and providing parents with information about child development;
- rehabilitation counselling;
- early identification and assessment of disabilities in children;
- school health services provided by a school nurse or other qualified personnel;
- social work services; and
- social work services in school, including group and individual counseling with the child and family, working with problems in a child's home, school or community that affect his or her adjustment in school, and mobilizing school and community resources to enable the child to receive maximum benefit from his or her educational program.[33]

These services are *not* the only ones that qualify as related services: if a child needs a particular service in order to benefit from special education and the service is a developmental, supportive or corrective one, it is also a "related" one and should be provided regardless of whether it is expressly listed in IDEA or its regulations.[34] For some children, for example, a part or full time aide might constitute a required related service,[35] as might certain equipment or assistive technology, such as a computer or tape recorder.[36]

Section 504 regulations do not define the "related aids and services" required for §504 compliance. However, as is the case with the "special education" component of a free appropriate education, related services developed and delivered in accordance with IDEA dictates will ordinarily satisfy the §504 requirement as well.[37]

D. Integration to the Maximum Extent Appropriate:
Least Restrictive Environment / Mainstreaming Requirements

IDEA requires that a student's IEP be implemented in a setting that allows him or her to be integrated into the regular education setting to the maximum extent consistent with his or her needs. The statute compels states and school systems to ensure that:

    "to the *maximum extent appropriate*, children with disabilities, including children in public or private institutions or other care facilities, are educated with children who are not disabled, and that special classes, separate schooling, or other removal of children with disabilities from the regular education environment occurs only when the nature or severity of the disability is such that education in regular classes *with the use of supplementary aids and services* cannot be achieved satisfactorily."[38]

In addition, school systems must place children with disabilities in the same schools they would have attended if not disabled unless a student's IEP requires some other arrangement.[39] The §504 regulations impose similar requirements, calling for placement in the regular education environment unless the school district can demonstrate that "the education of...[a particular student] in the regular environment with the use of supplementary aids and services cannot be achieved satisfactorily."[40] If a child is to be placed in a setting *other* than regular education, the distance between the alternative program and the child's home must be taken into account.[41]

Both statutes also require school systems to ensure that each child with disabilities participates in mainstream non-academic and extra-curricular activities, including meals and recess periods, "to the maximum extent appropriate to the needs of" that child.[42] The §504 regulations additionally state that school systems "shall provide non-academic and extracurricular services and activities in such manner as is necessary to afford handicapped students an equal opportunity for participation in such services and activities."[43] IDEA regulations impose the same requirement.[44]

In addition to protecting the right of children with disabilities to participate in regular education classes and activities, the maximum appropriate integration requirement protects children whose needs cannot be met in regular education classes from overly restrictive and isolated placements. Thus, for example, IDEA and §504 integration requirements would be violated if a child who could be educated appropriately in a special education classroom within a "regular" education elementary school were nonetheless placed in a segregated school for children with disabilities.[45]

A school district proposing to remove a child from the mainstream bears the burden of proving that such an exclusion from the regular education setting — whether total or partial — is justifiable in view of the above-described requirements.[46] School districts must thus assess the extent to which, given appropriate supports, a child may be educated in the regular education setting before attempting a more restrictive placement.[47] Such supports might include, but are not limited to, provision of a classroom aide,[48] use of computers or other assistive technology,[49] modification of the regular education curriculum, or time in a resource room or the services of an itinerant special education teacher in conjunction with regular education classes.[50]

This same individualized assessment of maximum appropriate integration — including participation in meals, recess and other non-academic activities — should also be made in determining how restrictive a placement is appropriate for a child who cannot be served in a regular education classroom.[51]

IDEA prohibits a school district from excluding a child with disabilities from the regular education setting simply because it disagrees philosophically with integration or mainstreaming as an educational method,[52] and from denying mainstreaming simply because the child cannot learn or perform at the same level as his or her prospective regular education classmates.[53] Rather, each child's unique educational needs and the benefits mainstreaming will afford him or her must be assessed on an individual basis.

E. The Meaning of "Free":
Using Social Security, SSI Benefits or Private Insurance to Pay for Services Required Under IDEA or §504

Because both IDEA and §504 require that special education and related services be "free" — meaning provided at no cost to children with disabilities, their parents or guardians — parents cannot be required to use their child's social security or SSI benefits to fund services owed them under these statutes.[54] For the same reason, school districts may not require a parent to use private health insurance to pay for or defray the cost of special education and/or related services if use of the insurance poses a risk of financial loss to parent or child.[55]

It is not necessarily improper for school officials or others providing services required under IDEA or §504 to *ask* parents to use their health insurance benefits. However, a school system seeking to bill private insurance or otherwise use insurance proceeds must provide the parent with information regarding the ways in which financial loss might result *and* explain that use of insurance is voluntary. And if a parent refuses to use his or her private insurance, the school district must still provide the required service.[56] This is the case regardless of the reason behind a parent's refusal.[57]

Financial loss from the use of insurance may occur in many ways, including:

- a decrease in available lifetime coverage under the policy;
- a decrease in available annual coverage or any other benefit under the policy;
- payment of a deductible amount for a particular service;
- an increase in premiums;
- discontinuation of the policy; and
- decreased future insurability with a different insurance company if the educational services for which insurance is used are deemed treatment for a pre-existing medical condition.[58]

The U.S. Department of Education's Office of Civil Rights ("OCR"), which enforces §504, and its Office of Special Education Programs ("OSEP"), which enforces IDEA, have both held that all of the above pose a realistic threat of financial loss such that parents need not consent to the use of insurance.[59]

Notes

1. 20 U.S.C. §1401(a)(18).

2. 34 C.F.R. §104.33(b).

3. *See* 20 U.S.C. §§1412(5)(b) and 1414(a)(1)(c)(iv); 34 C.F.R. §§300.550 through 300.556; 34 C.F.R. §104.34.

4. 20 U.S.C. §1401(a)(18)(D); Board of Education of the Hendrick Hudson Central School District v. Rowley, 458 U.S. 176, 206 n.27, 102 S.Ct. 3034, 3051 n.27 (1982).

5. 20 U.S.C. §1401(a)(20); 34 C.F.R. §300.346.

6. *See* Timothy W. v. Rochester School District, 875 F.2d 954, 973 (1st. Cir. 1989), *cert. denied*, 110 S. Ct. 519 ("...educational methods...are not static, but are constantly evolving and improving. It is the school district's responsibility to avail itself of these new approaches in providing an education program geared to each child's individual needs"); *see also* 20 U.S.C. §1413(a)(3)(B) (state plan required by IDEA must include procedures for, *inter alia*, acquiring and disseminating to teachers, administrators and related services personnel significant knowledge derived from education research and other sources, and adopting, where appropriate, promising practices, materials and technology); 34 C.F.R. §300.385 (requiring states to have in place a statewide system designed to adopt, where appropriate,

promising educational practices and materials shown to be effective through research and demonstration and to provide for thorough reassessment of the educational practices used in the state).

7. 34 C.F.R. §104.33(b)(2).

8. 20 U.S.C. §1401(a)(18).

9. *Id.*

10. 458 U.S. 176, 102 S.Ct. 3034 (1982).

11. 458 U.S. at 206-207, 102 S.Ct. at 305.

12. Board of Education of East Windsor Regional School District v. Diamond, 808 F.2d 987, 991 (3rd Cir. 1986) (emphasis in original); *see also* Cordrey v. Euckert, 917 F.2d 1460, 1473 (6th Cir. 1990), *cert. denied*, 111 S. Ct. 1391 (1991) (child must benefit meaningfully within his or her potential); Doe v. Smith, 879 F.2d 1340, 1341 (6th Cir. 1989), *cert. denied*, 110 S. Ct. 730 (1990) (benefit must be more than *de minimis*); Polk v. Central Susquehanna Intermediate Unit 16, 853 F.2d 171, 184-85 (3rd Cir. 1988), *cert. denied* 109 S.Ct. 838 (*de minimis* or trivial benefit insufficient; whether benefit is *de minimis* must be gauged in relation to child's potential); Hall v. Vance County Board of Education, 774 F.2d 629, 636 (4th Cir. 1985) ("[c]learly, Congress did not intend that a school system could discharge its duty...by providing a program that produces some minimal academic advancement, no matter how trivial"); Johnson v. Lancaster-Lebanon Intermediate Unit 13, 757 F. Supp. 606, 618 (E.D. Penn. 1991) (educational program must be sufficient for student to make "meaningful educational progress"); Chris D. v. Montgomery County Board of Education, 743 F. Supp. 1524, 1531 (M.D.Ala. 1990) (rejecting implicit school board contention that "a benefit is conferred anytime a student is not left to vegetate"); *cf.* Alamo Heights Independent School District v. State Board of Education, 790 F.2d 1153, 1158 (5th Cir. 1986).

13. 458 U.S. at 200, 102 S.Ct. at 3048.

14. Town of Burlington v. Department of Education, 736 F.2d 773, 788 (1st Cir. 1984), *aff'd.*, 471 U.S. 359, 105 S.Ct. 1996 (1985).

15. Massachusetts, for example, requires educational services designed to benefit a child with disabilities "to the maximum extent feasible." Mass. Gen. Laws c. 71B, §3.

16. 20 U.S.C. §1401(a)(18)(B); 34 C.F.R. §300.4(b).

17. *Town of Burlington*, 736 F.2d at 789; Johnson v. Independent School District No. 4, 921 F.2d 1022, 1029 (10th Cir. 1990), *cert. denied*, 59 U.S.L.W. 3741 (1991); Thomas v. Cincinnati Board of Education, 918 F.2d 618, 620 (6th Cir. 1990); Geis v. Board of Education of Persippany-Troy Hills, 774 F.2d 575, 581 (3rd Cir. 1985); Students of California School for the Blind v. Honig, 736 F.2d 538, 544-545 (9th Cir. 1984), *vacated as moot*, 471 U.S. 148, 105 S.Ct. 1928; Pink v. Mt. Diablo Unified School District, 738 F. Supp. 345, 346-347 (N.D. Cal. 1990); Barwacz v. Michigan Department of Education, 674 F. Supp. 1296, 1303-1304 (W.D. Mich. 1987).

18. 34 C.F.R. §300.305.

19. Comment to 34 C.F.R. §300.305.

20. 34 C.F.R. §300.307(a).

21. 34 C.F.R. §104.33(b)(1)(i).

22. 34 C.F.R. §104.33(b)(2).

23. 34 C.F.R. §104.33(b)(1)(ii).

24. 34 C.F.R. §§104.4(b)(ii) and (iii).

25. South Central (IN) Area Special Education Cooperative, 17 EHLR 248, 250 (OCR 9/25/90); *see also* East Baton Rouge (LA) Parish School System, EHLR 353:252, :255 (OCR 6/14/89); Tippecanoe (IN) School Corporation, EHLR 353:217 (OCR 6/14/88).

26. 34 C.F.R. §104.34(c).

27. 20 U.S.C. §1401(a)(16) (emphasis added). The term special education "includes instruction conducted in the classroom, in the home, in hospitals and institutions, and in other settings," 20 U.S.C. §1401(a)(16)(A), as well as "instruction in physical education." 20 U.S.C. §1401(a)(16)(B).

28. *See, e.g.*, Board of Education of the County of Cabell v. Dienelt, 1986-87 EHLR DEC. [Education for the Handicapped Law Report Decisions] 558:305, :308 (S.D. W.Va. 1987) (school board failed to provide free appropriate public education when it attempted to place student with learning disabilities in its "generalized special education program without reference to the child's individualized needs"), *aff'd. per curiam,* 843 F.2d 813 (4th Cir. 1988).

29. *See* 34 C.F.R. §104.4(b)(1)(iv), which prohibits recipients of federal funds from providing different or separate services to people with disabilities or any category of people with disabilities unless such treatment is necessary to provide them services as effective as those provided to non-disabled people.

30. 20 U.S.C. §1401(a)(17).

31. *See, e.g.*, Inquiry of Rainforth, 17 EHLR 222 (OSEP 10/24/90) (regarding IDEA); Prescott (AZ) Unified School District No. 1, EHLR 352:540 (OCR 5/22/87) (regarding §504).

32. 34 C.F.R. §300.13(b)(13).

33. 20 U.S.C. §1401(a)(17) and 34 C.F.R. §300.13. Rehabilitation counseling services, social work services and therapeutic recreation were added to IDEA in 1990 and, as of this writing, were not yet included in the IDEA regulations. The Department of Education published proposed regulations including and defining these related services on August 19, 1991. See 56 Fed. Reg. 41271 (1991).

34. Comment to 34 C.F.R. §300.13.

35. *See, e.g.*, Thornock v. Boise Independent School District #1, 115 Idaho 466, 767 P.2d 1241 (1988), *cert. denied,* 109 S.Ct. 2069 (1989).

36. Depending upon a student's particular circumstances, a school system might be required to provide a computer or other assistive technology as "special education," as a "related service" or as a "supplementary aid or service" to facilitate his or her education in the regular education setting pursuant to IDEA's least restrictive environment requirements. Inquiry of Goodman, 16 EHLR 1317 (OSEP 8/10/90). The Department of Education published a proposed regulation in the August 19, 1991 Federal Register that would reiterate the existing school system obligation to provide assistive technology devices and assistive technology services to children who need them in order to receive a free appropriate public education. See 56 Fed. Reg. 41272 (1991). The 1990 amendments to IDEA added definitions of "assistive technology device" and "assistive technology services" to the statute, codified at 20 U.S.C. §§1401(a)(25) and (26).

37. 34 C.F.R. §104.33(b)(2).

38. 20 U.S.C. §1412(5)(B) (emphasis added); see also 34 C.F.R. §300.550.

39. 34 C.F.R. §300.552(c).

40. 34 C.F.R. §104.34(a). Section 504 also prohibits the provision of different or separate educational services to students with disabilities or to any class of students with disabilities unless those services are necessary to provide students with disabilities with services that are as effective as those provided to others. 34 C.F.R. §104.4(b)(iv).

41. 34 C.F.R. §104.34(a).

42. 34 C.F.R. §300.553; 34 C.F.R. §104.34(b).

43. 34 C.F.R. §104.37(a)(1).

44. 34 C.F.R. §300.306(a).

45. *See, e.g.,* Roncker v. Walter, 700 F.2d 1058 (6th Cir 1983), *cert. denied,* 464 U.S. 864, 104 S.Ct. 196.

46. Tokarcik v. Forest Hills School District, 665 F.2d 443, 458 (3rd Cir. 1981), *cert. denied,* 458 U.S. 1121; Davis v. District of Columbia Board of Education, 530 F. Supp. 1209, 1211-1212 (D.D.C. 1982); Mills v. Board of Education of the District of Columbia, 348 F. Supp. 866, 880-881 (D.D.C. 1972); 34 C.F.R. §104.34(a).

47. Daniel R. v. State Board of Education, 874 F.2d 1036, 1048 (5th Cir. 1989).

48. *See, e.g., Thornock, supra.*

49. Inquiry of Goodman, 16 EHLR 1317 (OSEP 8/10/90).

50. *See* 34 C.F.R. §300.551; *see also, e.g., Daniel R., supra.*

51. *See, e.g., Roncker, supra.*

52. *Roncker,* 700 F.2d at 1063, citing Campbell v. Talladega City Board of Education, 518 F. Supp. 47, 55 (N.D. Ala. 1981).

53. *Daniel R.,* 874 F.2d at 1047.

54. McLain v. Smith, 16 EHLR 6 (E.D. Tenn. 1989).

55. 20 U.S.C. §§1401(a)(16) and (18); 34 C.F.R. §§300.4, 300.14; 34 C.F.R. §104.33(c); Shook v. Gaston County Board of Education, 882 F.2d 119 (4th Cir. 1989), *cert. denied*, 58 U.S.L.W. 3528 (2/20/90); Seals v. Loftis, 614 F. Supp. 302 (E.D. Tenn. 1985); Inquiry of Simon, 17 EHLR 225 (OSEP 11/9/90); Trans Allied-Medical Services, Inc., 16 EHLR 963 (OCR 5/30/90); Inquiry of Stohrer, EHLR 213:211 (OSEP 2/24/89).

56. *Inquiry of Simon, supra; Inquiry of Stohrer, supra; Trans Allied-Medical Services, supra.*

57. *Inquiry of Simon, supra.*

58. *See Shook, supra; Seals, supra; Inquiry of Simon, supra; Trans Allied-Medical Education Services, supra.*

59. *Trans Allied-Medical Educational Services, supra; Inquiry of Simon, supra.*

III.

Special Issues Regarding Related Services:

The "Medical Exclusion," In-School Assistance with Health-Related Needs, and Children with Substance Abuse Problems or Psychiatric Disorders

A. The "Medical Exclusion" In General

As noted in the previous chapter, the IDEA definition of "related services" includes "medical services...for diagnostic and evaluation purposes only."[1] "Medical services," in turn, are defined in the IDEA regulations as "services provided by a licensed physician to determine a child's medically related handicapping condition which results in the child's need for special education and related services."[2] Physician services that are neither diagnostic nor evaluative are thus excluded from the group of related services school systems must provide.

Whether IDEA's medical exclusion excuses a school system from providing a particular service is not always clear. It is not always easy (or possible or even reasonable) to separate "education" from "treatment" or "educational" needs from health or "medical" ones. And because the definition of "medical services" found in the regulations refers to "services provided by a licensed physician," there has been disagreement about whether *only* services provided by a physician are "medical" — and therefore excluded — or whether services provided by others can be deemed excludable "medical" ones as well.[3] There has also been disagreement on the question of whether a specific service listed in IDEA or the regulations as a required related service becomes an excluded medical service simply because a physician happens to perform it.[4]

Finally, the difficulty in determining whether the medical exclusion applies in a given case is further complicated by the fact that, depending upon the service in question, other IDEA regulations, such as those regarding the provision of school health services and those governing the costs of residential placements, may come into play. These issues surface most frequently for students with disabilities whose health-related needs require substantial assistance in school, who have been diagnosed as having a psychiatric disorder, or who require treatment for alcohol or drug abuse.

B. Related Services for Children with Health-Related Needs Requiring Substantial Assistance in School

In *Irving Independent School District v. Tatro*,[5] the U.S. Supreme Court held that if a student cannot attend school unless provided with certain health-related assistance during the school day, such help is a "supportive service" necessary to assist him or her to benefit from special education. If the necessary health-related assistance can be provided by a school nurse, trained layperson or other non-physician, it is *not* an excludable medical service; rather, it is a "school health service" as defined by the IDEA regulations — and so a required related service under IDEA.[6]

In *Tatro*, the Supreme Court applied these principles to require a school district to provide clean intermittent catheterization to a student needing it every three to four hours during the school day.[7] Other courts have required services such as the suctioning and reinsertion of tracheostomy tubes.[8] In each of these cases, the courts found that the medical exclusion did not apply because, among other things, the service in question was not to be performed by a physician.

These same IDEA provisions and principles should apply to any other health-related assistance a child might require during the school day. Advocates should be aware, however, that two federal courts have ruled that IDEA does not require school systems to provide in-school, full-time, one-to-one nursing services: in both cases, the court ruled that such services fell within the medical exclusion even though not provided by a physician.[9] At least one other federal court has disagreed with this conclusion, stating that these two cases conflict with the Supreme Court's decision in *Tatro* and so were wrongly decided.[10]

Section 504 also requires school districts to assist students with disabilities whose health-related needs require attention during the school day. Under §504, a school district must take reasonable steps to accommodate a student's disability if necessary to permit him or her to attend school.[11] Required accommodations can include modifying school programs, providing the student with supplementary services and, as one court has held, providing health-related services such as clean intermittent catheterization.[12] The Supreme Court has placed limits on the duty to accommodate, however, ruling that §504 does not require accommodations that would impose "undue financial and administrative burdens" or entail "substantial adjustments in existing programs."[13]

C. Related Services for Children Diagnosed as Having a Psychiatric Disorder

A psychiatric disorder in and of itself does not automatically make a child eligible for special education and related services under IDEA. In order to fall within IDEA, he or she must also meet the criteria of one of its listed disabilities — such as "serious emotional disturbance" or "other health impairment" — and need special education and related services as a result.[14] For purposes of §504, a psychiatric disorder is likely to constitute a "mental impairment which substantially limits one or more major life activities"[15] entitling a child to §504 protections, especially if the condition has resulted in hospitalization.[16]

1. Residential Placement in Psychiatric Facilities and Schools

Disputes regarding related services for children diagnosed as having a psychiatric disorder seem to arise most often when a child needs a residential placement. The IDEA regulations provide that

> "[i]f placement in a public or private residential program is necessary to provide special education and related services to a handicapped child, the program, including *non-medical care* and room and board, must be at no cost to the parents of the child."[17]

A Department of Education comment to this regulation states that it applies to residential placements that are made "for educational purposes."[18] Relying upon this regulation and the "medical exclusion" explained above, some school systems have claimed that they need not fund residential placements in programs capable of addressing psychiatric needs because such placements are "medical" rather than "educational."

Different courts have made different decisions when presented with this argument. In some cases, school systems have been held responsible for the entire cost of the placement.[19] In at least one case, the court ruled that the school system would be held responsible for room and board and certain related services, including at least some psychotherapy, but not for other components of the program that the court might deem "medical."[20] In other cases, courts have ruled that the school system was *not* responsible for room and board and other costs the court deemed "medical," but *was* required to pay for tuition and certain related services such as (in some cases) counselling or psychotherapy.[21] In still others, courts have held that the school system was not responsible for any portion of the costs.[22]

In most of these cases, the court tried to determine whether the placement — and the individual services provided at the placement — addressed primarily "medical" needs or primarily "educational" ones. The following are some of the factors courts have taken into account in making this distinction:

- whether the initial reason for the placement was to treat an acute psychiatric crisis or episode of mental illness, or whether the student was medically stable at the time the placement was made or sought;[23]
- whether the residential facility was licensed or certified by state authorities as a special education facility;[24]
- the extent to which therapies, treatment or services were geared towards restoring the student's ability to function in school, improving school performance, or making school instruction more effective for the student in comparison to other goals of the therapies, treatment or services;[25]
- whether services provided in the residential program were implemented by way of an IEP developed by school personnel, or at least furthered IEP goals, or whether services were determined solely by a medical team on the basis of the team's perception of the student's treatment needs;[26] and
- whether the primary focus of the placement is on what the court deems "treatment" or "cure" of a psychiatric illness, or whether the primary focus is on providing special education instruction and services in a therapeutic setting.[27]

Regardless of whether a school district is responsible for providing a residential placement, it *must*, at a minimum, provide students hospitalized in psychiatric facilities with educational instruction during their hospital stay.[28]

2. Psychotherapy as a Related Service

Although psychotherapy is not specifically mentioned in the list of examples of "related services" contained in IDEA and its regulations, it has been recognized as a related service that school districts must provide if necessary to assist a child to benefit from special education.[29] Psychotherapy also falls within the IDEA definitions of "psychological services" and "counselling services," both of which appear in the regulations as examples of related services.[30]

Some courts have ruled that the "medical exclusion" excuses a school system from providing psychotherapy or counselling that it would otherwise be required to provide if the therapist or counselor is a psychiatrist.[31] Under this reasoning, a psychiatrist's status as a licensed physician automatically excludes all of his or her services except for diagnostic and evaluative services.

Other courts, however, have held that psychotherapy or counselling does not necessarily become an excludable medical service simply because it is provided by a psychiatrist.[32] Rather, the determination of whether the service is a required, related one or an excludable, medical one depends upon the nature and purpose of the service rather than the identity of the person providing it.[33]

D. Related Services for Students With Drug or Alcohol Abuse Problems

1. IDEA

Substance abuse or addiction in and of itself does not automatically make a student eligible for special education and related services under IDEA; to be eligible, he or she must fall within one of the disability categories listed in the statute and need special education and related services as a result. To date, OSEP has maintained that chemical dependence is *not* an "other health impairment" and so does not trigger IDEA eligibility, regardless of its affect on educational performance.[34] This interpretation has not yet been judicially challenged.

Even under OSEP's interpretation, however, *if a student is eligible for special education and related services under IDEA because of some **other** condition **and** has a substance abuse problem that interferes* *with his or her ability to benefit from special education, he or she is entitled to supportive, related services aimed at the substance abuse problem.* This is true even if the substance abuse "caused" the other disability, such as where, for example, an addicted child becomes "seriously emotionally disturbed" within the meaning of IDEA.[35]

Although the "medical exclusion" and the issues discussed above regarding services for children with psychiatric disorders may limit the particular substance abuse services school districts must provide, individual, group and family counselling and other psychological services provided by non-physicians are outside of the medical exclusion. They should, therefore, be provided if needed to enable the student to benefit from special education. Peer support groups along the lines of Alcoholics or Narcotics Anonymous might be another required service.

In addition and as explained in regard to children with psychiatric diagnoses, certain services provided by residential treatment programs — including the residential placement itself — might be required related services under IDEA despite the medical exclusion and despite school district attempts to classify them as "non-educational." OSEP has recognized that where a residential program is needed in order to provide an addicted and otherwise disabled child with a free appropriate public education, a residential program must be provided.[36]

2. § 504

Students who are addicted to drugs or alcohol *are* "individual[s] with handicaps" within the meaning of §504.[37] School districts therefore must conduct evaluations of addicted students, assess their individual educational needs and, based upon that assessment, provide a free appropriate public education consisting of special or regular education and related aids and services.[38] Thus, at a minimum, §504 requires school districts to provide the kind of substance abuse services described above in regard to IDEA. This is the case even if the student is not eligible for special education and related services under IDEA.[39]

Advocates should be aware that 1990 amendments to §504 made by the Americans with Disabilities Act[40] may allow schools to take disciplinary action against students currently using illegal drugs or alcohol for use or possession in a manner that would otherwise be prohibited by §504.[41] The 1990 amendments also exclude individuals who are "currently engaging in the illegal use of drugs" from the definition of "individual with handicaps" when action is taken "on the basis of such use."[42] The implications of this amendment for chemically dependent students are not yet clear.

Notes

1. 20 U.S.C. §1401(a)(17).

2. 34 C.F.R. §300.13(b)(4).

3. *E.g. compare* Irving Independent School District v. Tatro, 468 U.S. 883, 104 S.Ct. 3371 (1984) *with* Detsel v. Board of Education of Auburn Enlarged School District, 637 F. Supp. 1022 (N.D. N.Y. 1986), *aff'd. per curiam*, 820 F.2d 587 (2nd Cir. 1987), *cert. denied*, 108 S.Ct. 495.

4. *See, e.g.*, Tice v. Botentourt County School Board, 908 F.2d 1200, 1209 n.13 (4th Cir. 1990); Vander Malle v. Ambach, 667 F. Supp. 1015, 1042 (S.D.N.Y. 1987); Max M. v. Illinois State Board of Education, 629 F. Supp. 1504, 1519; Board of Education of the Town of Cheshire v. Department of Education, 17 EHLR 942 (Conn. Super. Ct. 1991).

5. 468 U.S. 883, 890, 104 S.Ct. 3371, 3376 (1984).

6. *Id.*, 468 U.S. at 892-893, 104 S.Ct. at 3377-3378.

7. *Id.*, 468 U.S. at 895, 104 S.Ct. at 3378. For an earlier case requiring a school district to provide clean intermittent catheterization as a related service, see Tokarcik v. Forest Hills School District, 665 F.2d 443 (3rd Cir. 1981), *cert. denied*, 458 U.S. 1121 (1982).

8. *See, e.g.*, Department of Education, State of Hawaii v. Katherine D., 727 F.2d 809 (9th Cir. 1983), *cert. denied*, 471 U.S. 1117 (1985); Macomb County Intermediate School District v. Joshua S., 715 F.Supp. 824 (E.D. Mich. 1989).

9. The two cases are Bevin H. v. Wright, 666 F. Supp. 71 (W.D. Pa. 1987), and *Detsel, supra*. The in-school nursing services needed by the student in *Detsel* were ultimately found to be covered by Medicaid. *See* Detsel v. Sullivan, 895 F.2d 58.(2nd Cir. 1990).

10. The case is *Macomb County Intermediate School District, supra*. For the court's criticism of *Detsel*, see 715 F. Supp. at 826-827. *But see also* Clovis Unified School District v. California Office of Administrative Hearings, 903 F.2d 635, 643-644 (9th Cir. 1990) (citing the *Detsel* analysis with approval).

11. Tatro v. State of Texas, 625 F.2d 557, 564-565 (5th Cir. 1980), *aff'd. on other grounds sub nom.*, Irving Independent School District v. Tatro, 468 U.S. 883, 104 S.Ct. 3371 (1984).

12. *Id.*, 625 F.2d at 564-565.

13. *Id.* at 564-565 n. 19, citing Southeastern Community College v. Davis, 99 S.Ct. 2361, 2369-2370 (1979).

14. *See* 20 U.S.C. §1401(a)(1). For definitions of "serious emotional disturbance" and "other health impairment," see 34 C.F.R. §300.5(b).

15. 29 U.S.C. §706(8)(B); 34 C.F.R. §104.3(j)(1).

16. *See. e.g.,* Community Unit School District #300 (IL) EHLR 353:296 (OCR 1989).

17. 34 C.F.R. §300.302 (emphasis added).

18. Comment to 34 C.F.R. §300.302.

19. *See, e.g.,* Papacoda v. State of Connecticut, 528 F. Supp. 68 (D. Ct. 1981).

20. *Vander Malle,* 667 F. Supp. at 1042.

21. *Tice, supra;* Taylor v. Honig, 910 F.2d 627 (9th Cir. 1990); Doe v. Anrig, 651 F. Supp. 424 (D. Mass. 1987;) McKenzie v. Jefferson, 566 F. Supp. 404 (D.D.C. 1983); Darlene L. v. Illinois State Board of Education, 568 F. Supp. 1340 (N.D. Ill. 1983).

22. Clovis Unified School District v. California Office of Administrative Hearings, 903 F.2d 635 (9th Cir. 1990); Los Gatos Joint Union High School District v. Doe, 1984-85 EHLR DEC. 556:281 (N.D.Cal. 1984); Metropolitan Government of Nashville and Davidson County v. Tennessee Department of Education, 1988-1989 EHLR DEC. 441:450 (Tenn. Ct. of App. 1989).

23. *Los Gatos, supra.; McKenzie, supra.; Papacoda, supra.; Metropolitan Government of Nashville-Davidson County, supra.; Tice, supra.; Clovis, supra.; Taylor, supra.*

24. *Anrig, supra.; Clovis, supra.; Taylor, supra.; Papacoda, supra.*

25. *Vander Malle, supra.; Los Gatos, supra.; Papacoda, supra.; Clovis, supra.*

26. *Clovis, supra.; Taylor, supra.; Anrig, supra.*

27. *Compare Los Gatos, supra.,* and *Clovis, supra.,* with *Papacoda, supra.*

28. *See* 20 U.S.C. §1401(a)(16) (defining "special education" to include instruction in hospitals).

29. *See, e.g., Clovis,* 903 F.2d at 645; *Max M.* 629 F. Supp. at 1519; T.G. v. Board of Education of Piscataway, 576 F. Supp. 420, 423 (D.N.J. 1983), *aff'd.* 738 F.2d 420 (3rd Cir.), *cert. denied,* 469 U.S. 1086, 105 S.Ct. 592 (1984); *Papacoda,* 528 F. Supp. at 72; *Anrig,* 651 F. Supp. at 430-431.

30. *Papacoda,* 528 F. Supp. at 72. For definitions of "psychological services" and "counseling" for purposes of IDEA, see 34 C.F.R. §300.5(b).

31. *See Darlene L., supra; McKenzie, supra; Metropolitan Government of Nashville and Davidson County, supra.*

32. *See Tice,* 908 F.2d at 1209 n.13; *Town of Cheshire, supra; see also Vander Malle,* 667 F. Supp. at 1042; *Max M.,* 629 F. Supp. at 1519 (where school district refused to provide psychotherapy and parents obtained service from psychiatrist at own expense, school district must reimburse up

to the amount it would have cost for a qualified non-psychiatrist to provide therapy).

33. *Tice*, 908 F.2d at 1209 n.13; *Town of Cheshire*, 17 EHLR at 942.

34. See Inquiry of Harris, EHLR 211:431 (OSEP 11/26/86).

35. *See, e.g.* Inquiry of Scariano, EHLR 213:133 (OSEP 4/18/88).

36. *Id.*

37. 34 C.F.R. Pt. 104, App. A, para. 4; Lake Washington School District No. 414, EHLR 257:611 (OCR 6/28/85); Northwest Kansas Area Vocational-Technical School, EHLR 353:190 (OCR 1/29/89).

38. 34 C.F.R. §§104.33 and 104.34; Lake Washington (WA) School District No. 414, EHLR 257:611 (OCR 6/28/85).

39. *Lake Washington School District #414, supra.*

40. Pub. L. 101-336, 104 Stat. 327.

41. The relevant changes were made by §512 of Pub. L. 101-336, 104 Stat. 327, amending 29 U.S.C. §706(8). For a discussion of discipline issues, see Chapter VIII, *infra.*

42. 29 U.S.C. §706(8)(C). This change was made by §512 of the 1990 Americans with Disabilities Act, Pub. L. 101-336, 104 Stat. 327, 376-77.

IV.
Educational Evaluations:
Rights, Procedures and Safeguards

A. Duty to Evaluate

Both IDEA and §504 require states and school systems to take affirmative steps to identify, locate and evaluate all children in the state or system who have disabilities and are in need of special education and related services.[1] Each also requires school systems to conduct a comprehensive, individual evaluation meeting certain criteria *before* placing any child in a special education program.[2]

How a child comes to be referred for an evaluation varies — as both a practical matter and a legal one — from state to state, and even from school district to school district. Many children are referred by their classroom teacher, others by their parents. IDEA simply requires states and school systems to identify and evaluate children who may have disabilities; it does not tell them how to do so. State law and regulations provide the specifics, including such details as who may make a referral, when and how a referral can be made and what, if any, steps should be taken to address a child's apparent difficulties before resorting to a referral for evaluation and special education.

The school system's legal duty to identify and evaluate students who need, or may need, special education or related services lasts for as long as the student remains of school age. Under IDEA, school systems must re-evaluate students with disabilities at least every three years, and more often than that if a child's individual needs so require, or if a parent or teacher requests an evaluation in the interim.[3] Section 504 prohibits school systems from making a "significant" change in a student's placement without first conducting a new evaluation.[4]

Both laws require an evaluation if a student's academic performance or behavior suddenly changes, whether or not the child has previously been identified as having disabilities and/or needing special education or related services.[5] In addition, OCR has ruled that psychiatric hospitalization should trigger an evaluation of a student's need for special or regular education and related services under §504.[6]

B. Protections in the Evaluation Process

Except for evaluations to determine whether a child has specific learning disabilities, neither IDEA nor §504 tell school systems *how* to perform the evaluations both laws require. Details such as the particular tests or other procedures that should be used to evaluate a child for a particular disability or the kind of expertise those performing particular evaluations should have are largely left to each state to regulate. Advocates should therefore review their own state's regulations and standards.

Both IDEA and §504 do, however, require state and local evaluation practices to meet certain minimum standards.

1. Notice and Consent

Notice A school system must give a parent prior written notice any time it proposes to conduct an evaluation.[7] Written notice is also required if the system refuses a parent's request for an evaluation.[8] These IDEA notice requirements apply to an initial, "preplacement" evaluation designed to determine whether a child needs special education as well as to subsequent evaluations and reevaluations.[9]

The IDEA regulations require that notice be written in language understandable to the general public and given to the parent in his or her native language.[10] In addition, they spell out detailed requirements governing the content of the notice.[11] These content requirements also apply to a number of other situations in which school districts must give prior written notice, and are discussed in Chapter VI.

Consent IDEA regulations require school systems to obtain parental consent before conducting an initial, "preplacement" evaluation and/or actually placing the child in special education for the first time.[12] The regulations also, however, permit school districts to conduct preplacement evaluations and make initial placements even where a parent does not consent. The procedures the district must follow in order to override a parent's refusal to consent depend upon whether *state* law, too, ordinarily requires parental consent.

If state law requires parental consent for preplacement evaluations and initial special education placement, the state's procedures for overriding a parent's refusal to consent, if any, will apply.[13] If state law does *not* require parental consent, the school district must seek (and prevail at) a due process hearing — described in Chapter VI, below — in order to proceed with the preplacement evaluation or initial special education placement over a parent's objection.[14]

The IDEA regulations do *not* require parental consent for subsequent evaluations. Some *state* statutes and regulations do require consent under such circumstances. However, IDEA regulations are ambiguous on the questions of whether such state rules are valid and whether a school district may conduct evaluations without consent once a child has already been placed in special education.[15] At a minimum, however, a parent objecting to a proposed evaluation that is not a preplacement evaluation has a right to challenge the district's plans by requesting a due process hearing.[16]

2. Criteria and Safeguards

Under IDEA, states and school systems must ensure that testing and evaluation procedures are not racially or culturally discriminatory.[17] IDEA evaluation standards also:

- require school systems to provide and administer tests and other evaluation materials in the child's native language or other primary way in which the child communicates;[18]
- prohibit school systems from using a single test or procedure as the basis for deciding that a child should be placed in a special education program or as the basis for designing a child's special education program;[19]
- require that evaluations be conducted by a multidisciplinary team or group of persons, including at least one teacher or specialist knowledgeable about the child's suspected area of disability;[20] and
- require school systems to assess a child in *all* areas related to the suspected disability, including health, vision, hearing, social and emotional status, general intelligence, academic performance, communication abilities and motor skills where appropriate.[21]

In addition, both IDEA and §504 require school systems to ensure:

- that tests and other evaluation materials have been proven valid for the specific purpose for which they are being used;
- that tests and other evaluation materials are administered by trained people following the instructions provided by the producer of the test or other evaluation materials;
- that the tests and other evaluation materials they use include

methods designed to assess specific areas of educational need and *not* just IQ; and

• that test results of children with impaired hearing or vision or manual or speaking skills actually reflect the child's aptitude rather than simply reflecting the fact that his or her vision, hearing, speaking skills or manual skills are impaired.[22]

3. Special Procedures for Evaluating Students Suspected of Having Specific Learning Disabilities

The standards described above apply to all evaluations, regardless of the student's disability or suspected disability. Additional IDEA requirements apply when a school system evaluates a student it suspects has a specific learning disability ("SLD").

First, the multidisciplinary team required for all evaluations must, in the case of SLD, include the child's regular teacher and at least one person qualified to conduct individual diagnostic tests of children (such as a school psychologist, speech-language pathologist or remedial reading teacher).[23] If the child does not have a regular teacher, the team must include instead a regular classroom teacher qualified to teach a child of his or her age; and if he or she is younger than school age, an individual qualified under state standards to teach a child of that age must be on the team.[24]

As part of the evaluation, at least one member of the team other than the child's regular teacher must observe his or her academic performance in the classroom. If the child is not in school, whether because he or she is too young or for some other reason, a team member must observe him or her in a setting appropriate for the child's age.[25]

The team may determine that a child has a specific learning disability if:

(1) when provided with learning experiences appropriate for his or her age and ability, the child does not achieve what would be expected for someone of his or her age and ability in
  • oral expression, or
  • listening comprehension, or
  • written expression, or
  • basic reading skill, or
  • reading comprehension, or

- mathematics calculation, or
- mathematics reading,

  AND

(2) the team finds that there is a "severe discrepancy" between the child's intellectual ability and what he or she is actually achieving in one or more of these listed areas.[26]

Neither IDEA nor its regulations define "severe discrepancy"; whether a severe discrepancy exists is determined by state law and standards.[27]

The team may *not* label a child as having a specific learning disability if the "severe discrepancy" between intellectual ability and actual achievement results from environmental, cultural or economic disadvantage; a visual, hearing, or motor impairment; mental retardation; or emotional disturbance.[28] The team's evaluation results must be presented in a written report[29] that states and explains:

- whether the child has a specific learning disability;
- the basis for the determination that the child does or does not have a specific learning disability;
- the behavior noted during the required observation of the child;
- the relationship between the behavior observed and the child's academic functioning;
- any educationally relevant medical findings;
- whether there is a "severe discrepancy" between achievement and ability that cannot be corrected unless the child is provided with special education and related services; and
- the team's determination concerning the role of environmental, cultural or economic disadvantage in any difference between the child's achievement and his or her ability.[30]

In addition, each team member must state whether he or she agrees or disagrees with the report's conclusions.[31] A team member who disagrees must submit a written statement presenting his or her own conclusions.[32]

C. Interpretation and Use of Evaluation Results

Evaluation results will be used first to determine whether the child has a disability and meets IDEA and/or §504 eligibility criteria. If so, they will then be used to develop educational goals and objectives, design special education instruction, decide upon the educational setting in which the child will be placed, and determine what kind of related aids and services will be necessary.

School systems may not use any single test or evaluation tool (such an IQ test) as the sole basis for determining whether a child has a disability and needs special education, or for determining what will constitute an appropriate educational program for him or her.[33] In interpreting and using evaluation results, school systems must:

*   draw upon information from a variety of sources, including aptitude and achievement tests, teacher recommendations, physical condition, social or cultural background and adaptive behavior;[34]

    [*Note:* The required social and cultural information should include information concerning health (including sleep, nutrition and housing); family structure, educational background and native language; access to books; and exposure to the kind of information and experiences tests assume and to test administrators.[35]]

*   ensure that information obtained from all of these sources is carefully documented and considered;[36] and

*   ensure that people knowledgeable about the meaning of the evaluation data participate in decisions regarding the child's educational program.[37]

Many of the tests and other procedures used in educational evaluations have been criticized by educators, psychologists, researchers and others as invalid for the purposes they are intended to serve, as racially or culturally biased, or as inaccurate for other reasons. Tests or other evaluation tools appropriate for some children may be inappropriate — and produce misleading results — for others. A great deal has been written on this subject, and advocates should be prepared to scrutinize this issue carefully, particularly if the parent's assessment of the child differs from that of the evaluation team and/or the child is a member of a racial, ethnic or linguistic minority.

Parents and their authorized representatives have the right to inspect, review and obtain copies of the tests administered as well as the test results and any other documents pertaining to testing/and or evaluation of their child.[38] This right includes the right to ask school personnel to explain and interpret these records, and to receive a response.[39]

D. Right to an Independent Educational Evaluation

1. Independent Evaluations at Private Expense

A parent who disagrees with an evaluation conducted by (or for) a school system, or who simply wants a second opinion, always has the right to obtain a second, "independent educational evaluation" — that is, a second evaluation performed by someone who is not employed by the school system — at parental expense, or at the expense of an agreeable evaluator or other outside party. School systems must take the results of any such evaluation into account when making decisions about the child's education.[40]

2. Independent Evaluations at Public Expense

Under certain circumstances, parents also have a right to an independent evaluation at *public expense* — most commonly the school system's.[41] Parents disagreeing with a school-conducted or school-initiated evaluation have a *right* to an independent one at public expense *unless* the school system requests a due process hearing (described in Chapter VI) and then proves that its own evaluation was "appropriate."[42] This right exists *each time* the school system conducts an evaluation, regardless of whether it is an initial preplacement evaluation or a three-year or more frequent re-evaluation.[43]

Often state regulations and/or individual school systems require an independent evaluation to meet certain criteria if the school system is to pay for it. Any criteria imposed by a local school system must be based upon state-wide standards adopted by the state education agency.[44] *Parents and advocates should check these local and state requirements before obtaining an evaluation.* Parents and advocates should also check to see if their state statute or regulations provide more liberal access to publicly-funded independent evaluations than does IDEA. Regardless of local or state requirements, if a school's evaluation involved classroom observation the independent evaluator, too, must be given access to the classroom.[45]

IDEA prohibits a state or school system from applying stricter criteria to independent evaluations than it applies to evaluations conducted or initiated by school systems.[46] IDEA itself says nothing about the kind, if any, of restrictions states and local school systems may place on publicly-funded evaluations — or even their authority to do so. The IDEA regulations state only that:

> "Whenever an independent evaluation is at public expense, the criteria under which the evaluation is obtained, including *the location of the evaluation and the qualifications of the examiner*, must be the same as the criteria which the public agency uses when it initiates an evaluation."[47]

OSEP, however, has taken the position that states and school systems may also set a ceiling on the cost of independent evaluations, subject to two conditions. First, the maximum fee must allow parents to choose among the various evaluators in the area qualified to conduct the specific test or procedure in question, eliminating only "unreasonably excessive" fees; districts cannot simply calculate the average of fees charged by various evaluators in the area for a particular procedure and declare that the maximum.[48] In addition, districts must waive the cost criteria and pay for a more expensive evaluation where a child's unique circumstances so require.[49]

OSEP has also stated that districts may "impose restrictions on the use of particular evaluators who had earlier been found by the district to be unsatisfactory."[50] A restriction of this sort, however, might dilute the right to an independent evaluation — and so, perhaps, violate IDEA — by allowing a school district to veto a parent's choice of evaluator if, for example, it disagreed with the evaluator's educational philosophy or feared that he or she would make recommendations expensive to implement. Advocates, however, should be aware of OSEP's position as well as the fact that this issue has not been decisively addressed by the courts.

Parents do *not* have to obtain school system approval before obtaining an independent evaluation, or even notify the school system in advance.[51] However, parents obtaining an independent evaluation without a school system commitment to pay for it run the risk that the system will later request a hearing and attempt to prove that it need not pay for the already-completed independent evaluation because its own evaluation was "appropriate." In addition, parents proceeding without first conferring with the school system run the risk that the evaluation they obtain will not meet whatever criteria the school system may legitimately impose, and so the risk that they will not be entitled to payment for that reason as well.

Parents without the resources to advance the money for an independent evaluation will usually not be able to obtain one unless the school system agrees in advance to pay. If the school system does *not* agree to pay and does *not* seek the hearing necessary to excuse it from paying, the parent has a "right" to an evaluation but no way to take advantage of that right. In response to this problem, OSEP has taken the position that a school system violates IDEA if it fails to *either* agree to pay *or* request a hearing for "so long as to essentially eliminate a parent's right to an" independent evaluation.[52]

A parent faced with this situation has a right to file a complaint and request a due process hearing in order to compel the school system to fund the evaluation. At the hearing, the *school system* will have the burden of proving that its evaluation was appropriate and that it therefore does not have to pay for another one.[53] The same complaint and hearing rights apply if the independent evaluation has already been performed and the school system refuses to reimburse the parent for it. Complaint and hearing procedures for these and all other IDEA disputes are explained in Chapter VI, below.

Finally, advocates should note that under IDEA, a hearing officer in a due process hearing involving the content of a child's education program may request an independent evaluation in order to assist him or her in making a decision.[54] Parents cannot be charged for an evaluation requested by a hearing officer as part of a hearing; the evaluation must be provided at public expense.[55] Advocates for parents unable to pay for an independent evaluation and unsuccessful in convincing the school district to do so might consider asking that the hearing officer request an evaluation. It is important to check any state regulations on this issue, as IDEA *allows* hearing officers to request independent evaluations but does not require them to do so.

Notes

1. 20 U.S.C. §§1412(2)(c) and 1414(a)(1)(A); 34 C.F.R. §§300.128 and 300.220; 34 C.F.R. §104.32.

2. 34 C.F.R. §300.531; 34 C.F.R. §104.35(a).

3. 34 C.F.R. §300.534(b).

4. 34 C.F.R. §104.35(a).

5. 34 C.F.R. 300.534(b); 34 C.F.R. §104.35(a) as interpreted by OCR in School Administrative Unit 19 (NH), 16 EHLR [Education for the Handicapped Law Report] 86 (OCR 1/4/89)(poor academic performance should trigger evaluation); Mineral County (NV) School District, 16 EHLR 668 (OCR 3/16/90) (inappropriate and/or disruptive behavior should trigger evaluation).

6. Community Unit School District #300 (IL), EHLR 353:296 (OCR 1989).

7. 34 C.F.R. §300.504(a).

8. *Id.*

9. *Id.*

10. 34 C.F.R. §300.505(b).

11. See 34 C.F.R. 300.505.

12. 34 C.F.R. §300.504.

13. 34 C.F.R. §300.504(c)(1).

14. 34 C.F.R. §300.504(c)(2).

15. This ambiguity is created by 34 C.F.R. §300.504(b)(2), which provides that "[e]xcept for preplacement evaluation and initial placement, consent may not be required as a condition of any benefit to the parent or child." The U.S. Department of Education/Office of Special Education Programs has taken the position that states may, consistent with IDEA, require parental consent for re-evaluations. If they do, however, according to OSEP they must also have procedures in place for overriding a parent's refusal to consent to reevaluation. See Inquiry of Crane, 17 EHLR 526 (OSEP 2/25/91); Inquiry of Conway, 17 EHLR 284 (OSEP 11/9/90). The Department of Education published a proposed new regulation reflecting this position in the August 19, 1991 Federal Register. See 56 Fed. Reg. 41274. IDEA itself does not address the circumstances, if any, under which a state or school district can evaluate a child over a parent's objection. Neither the existing regulation on consent nor OSEP's position on more protective state consent requirements has been judicially challenged.

16. 34 C.F.R. §300.506(a).

17. 20 U.S.C. §1412(5)(C); 34 C.F.R. §300.530(b). Racially discriminatory testing and evaluation methods may also violate Title VI of the Civil Rights Act of 1964, 42 U.S.C. §2000d *et seq.*

18. 34 C.F.R. §§300.532(a) and (b).

19. 34 C.F.R. §300.532(d).

20. 34 C.F.R. §300.532(e).

21. 34 C.F.R. §300.532(f).

22. 34 C.F.R. §§300.532(a) and (b); 34 C.F.R. §104.35(b).

23. 34 C.F.R. §300.540.

24. 34 C.F.R. §300.540.

25. 34 C.F.R. §300.542.

26. 34 C.F.R. §300.541(a).

27. *See* Inquiry of Scovill, EHLR 211:14 (Bureau of Education of the Handicapped [a predecessor of OSEP] 3/3/78). OCR has ruled that under §504, if the team believes that a student has a learning disability, its determination must prevail even if the student's test scores do not fall within the state formula for "severe discrepancy." *See* Georgia Department

of Education, EHLR 352:05 (OCR 5/20/85).

28. 34 C.F.R. §300.541(b).

29. 34 C.F.R. §300.543(a).

30. 34 C.F.R. §300.543(b).

31. 34 C.F.R. §300.543(c).

32. *Id.*

33. 34 C.F.R. §300.532(d); 34 C.F.R. §104.35.

34. 34 C.F.R. §300.533(a)(1); 34 C.F.R. §104.35(c)(1).

35. American Educational Research Assn., American Psychological Assn. and National Council on Measurement in Education, Standards for Educational and Psychological Testing (1985).

36. 34 C.F.R. §300.533(a)(2); 34 C.F.R. §104.35(c)(2).

37. 34 C.F.R. §300.533(a)(3); 34 C.F.R. §104.35(c)(3).

38. 34 C.F.R. §300.502 and 300.562.

39. 34 C.F.R. §300.562(b)(1).

40. 34 C.F.R. §300.503(c)(1).

41. 20 U.S.C. §1415(b)(1)(A);34 C.F.R. §300.503.

42. 34 C.F.R. §300.503(b).

43. Inquiry of Wilson, 16 EHLR 83 (OSEP 10/17/90); Inquiry of Thorne, 16 EHLR 606 (OSEP 2/15/90).

44. *See* Inquiry of Bluhm, EHLR 211:227 (OSEP 7/2/80).

45. *See* 34 C.F.R. §300.503(e), which provides that "whenever an independent evaluation is at public expense, the criteria under which the evaluation is obtained, including the location of the evaluation and the qualifications of the examiner, must be the same as the criteria which the public agency uses when it initiates an evaluation."

46. 34 C.F.R. §300.503(e); Inquiry of Rambo, 16 EHLR 1078 (OSEP 6/22/90).

47. 34 C.F.R. §300.503(e) (emphasis added).

48. *Inquiry of Wilson, supra; Inquiry of Thorne, supra; Inquiry of Fields, supra.*

49. *Inquiry of Wilson, supra; Inquiry of Thorne, supra; Inquiry of Fields, supra.*

50. *Inquiry of Bluhm*, EHLR at 211:229.

51. Hudson v. Wilson, 828 F.2d 1059 (4th Cir. 1987); Mullen v. District of Columbia, 16 EHLR 792 (D.D.C. 1990); Hiller v. Board of Education of the Brunswick Central School District, 687 F. Supp. 735 (N.D.N.Y. 1988).

52. Inquiry of Wessels, 16 EHLR 735 (OSEP 3/9/90); Inquiry of Smith, 16 EHLR 1080 (OSEP 6/28/90).

53. 34 C.F.R. §300.503(b); *Inquiry of Wilson, supra.*

54. 34 C.F.R. §300.504(d).

55. *Id.*

V.
IEPs, Placement Decisions and Parent Participation

All children eligible for special education and related services under IDEA must have an Individualized Education Program (IEP) *before* special education and related services begin.[1] Failure to develop an IEP — as well as failure to follow the specific procedures set out in IDEA and the regulations for doing so — is a failure to provide a free appropriate public education.[2] The §504 regulations do not require an IEP; however, provision of special education and related services under an IEP meeting IDEA criteria is one way of providing the appropriate education §504 requires.[3]

The IEP is more than a blueprint for the education a child is to receive. School districts *must* provide all services contained in the IEP, and violate IDEA if they fail to do so.[4]

A. IEP Components

By definition, an IEP must include the following:

- A statement of the child's present level of educational performance;[5]

    [*Note:* This statement should describe the effect of the child's disability on both academic (e.g. reading, communication) and non-academic (e.g. activities of daily living, mobility) aspects of his or her performance.[6] It should be written in objective, measurable terms, drawing upon evaluation results.[7]]

- A statement of annual goals, including short-term instructional objectives;[8]

    [*Note:* All problems noted in the statement of present educational performance should have corresponding annual goals and short-term instructional objectives.[9] Annual goals describe what the student can reasonably be expected to accomplish over a twelve-month period; short-term objectives should be measurable, intermediate steps towards the corresponding annual goal.[10]

Goals and objectives provide a basis for determining whether a child is progressing in, and benefitting from, his or her educational program, and so whether she or he is receiving an appropriate education.[11] The development of specific, measurable, well-defined, meaningful goals and objectives is crucial.]

- Objective criteria, evaluation procedures and schedules for determining, at least annually, whether the child is achieving the short term instructional objectives set out in the IEP;[12]
- A description of all of the specific educational services (specialized instruction and related services) to be provided;[13]
- The beginning date, amount and duration of each educational service to be provided;[14]

    [*Note:* The IEP should indicate whether the child will receive "extended year services" (summer or other programming beyond the standard school year) and/or "extended day services" (residential or other programming beyond the length of the standard school day). Like all other educational decisions under IDEA, determinations as to whether a student will receive extended year or day programming must be made on an individual basis in view of his or her unique needs.[15]]

- A description of the extent to which the child will participate in regular education programs (both academic and non-academic), including any supplementary aids and services necessary for participation in regular education;[16]
- For students aged 16 and up (and at age 14 or younger where appropriate), a statement of the transition services the student will need before leaving the public education system for adult living.[17] IDEA defines "transition services" as:

    "...a coordinated set of activities for a student, designed with an outcome-oriented process, which promotes movement from school to post-school activities, including post-secondary education, vocational training, integrated employment (including supported employment), continuing and adult education, adult services, independent living or community participation..."[18]

In addition, transition services must be based upon individual needs, take the student's interests and preferences into account and include instruction, community experiences, the development of employment and other post-school adult living objectives and, where appropriate, acquisition of daily living skills and functional vocational evaluation.[19]

The statement of transition services must specify whether agencies other than the school system will be involved in providing the services and, if so, describe their responsibilities.[20] If such a participating agency fails to provide agreed upon services, the school system must reconvene the IEP team and develop another strategy for meeting the student's transition objectives.[21]

B. IEP Process — Meetings and Parent Participation

IEPs must be developed *at a meeting* (or meetings) attended by the child's teacher, one or both parents, and a representative of the school system other than the child's teacher who is qualified to provide or supervise the provision of special education.[22] *This school system representative must have the authority to commit the school system to provide whatever services are included in the IEP so that the IEP will not be "vetoed" by school administrators or other school officials.*[23]

Whenever appropriate, the child, too, must be afforded the opportunity to attend the IEP meeting.[24] For a child who has been evaluated as needing special education and related services for the first time, meeting participants must also include a member of the evaluation team or some other individual who is knowledgeable about the evaluation procedures used and their results.[25] Parents and school districts may invite other individuals at their discretion.[26]

It is impermissible — and violates IDEA — for school personnel to present a completed IEP to parents for their approval at the meeting.[27] The IEP must be developed at the meeting, with parents afforded the opportunity to participate as full-fledged collaborators in designing their child's education.[28]

School systems are responsible for initiating IEP meetings and ensuring that parents are given a meaningful opportunity to attend and participate.[29] Towards this end, school districts must schedule the meeting at a mutually convenient time and place; notify parents of the meeting far enough in advance to ensure that they will have an opportunity to attend; and include in the notice of the meeting the purpose, time and location and a list of those who will attend.[30]

If neither parent can attend, the school district must use other methods to insure that parents participate in the development of the IEP, including individual or conference telephone calls.[31] A meeting can be held without a parent only if school personnel cannot convince the parents that they should attend.[32] Even then, the school system must first try to arrange a mutually agreeable time and place and must keep records of its efforts to do so.[33]

Parents have a right under IDEA to tape record IEP meetings.[34] Parents who themselves have disabilities and so are protected from discrimination under §504 may be entitled to certain accommodations at IEP meetings, including sign language interpreters provided at school district expense.[35]

C. Placement Decisions

Once a child's needs have been identified and corresponding services, goals and objectives developed through the IEP process, a placement capable of providing those services and achieving those goals and objectives can be selected. Placement decisions must be based upon the IEP.[36] *This means that the IEP must be developed* ***before*** *a placement is chosen.*[37] *A school system violates IDEA if it writes an IEP to fit a placement it has already selected.*[38]

Placements must be determined annually, must provide for maximum appropriate integration with non-disabled peers (as described in Chapter II) and must be as close to the child's home as possible.[39]

D. IEP Review and Revision

1. Periodic or Annual Reviews

School districts must periodically initiate and conduct meetings to review and, if appropriate, revise a child's IEP.[40] IEP review meetings should be held as often as necessary to address the child's needs.[41] At least one review meeting must be held each year.[42] The above-described requirements regarding meeting participants, meeting notice and parent participation rights apply to IEP review meetings as well.[43]

2. Revisions

Once an IEP has been developed and agreed upon, school personnel may not unilaterally change it. In order to revise an IEP or change a placement, school systems must follow the meeting and team process described above.[44] They must also give parents prior written notice of the proposed change.[45]

The IDEA regulations set out detailed requirements governing the content of this notice,[46] which also must be given any time a school system proposes or refuses to initiate or change the identification, evaluation, or educational placement of a child or the provision of a free appropriate public education to a child.[47] These content requirements are discussed in Chapter VI, below.

Parents may request an IEP or placement change, or a meeting to consider making a change, at any time. School districts should grant any reasonable request for an IEP meeting.[48] When a district refuses to make a change sought by a parent, it must provide the written notice described above. Parents may challenge any refusal to modify an IEP or change a placement by using the complaint and hearing procedures described in the following chapter.

Notes

1. 34 C.F.R. §300.342(b)(1).

2. 20 U.S.C. §1401(a)(18)(D); Board of Education of the Hendrick Hudson Central School District v. Rowley, 458 U.S. 176, 206-207, 102 S.Ct. 3034, 3035 (1982).

3. 34 C.F.R. §104.33(b)(2).

4. 20 U.S.C. §1401(a)(18); 34 C.F.R. §300.349; 34 C.F.R. part 300, App. C, para. 45.

5. 20 U.S.C. §1401(a)(20)(A).

6. 34 C.F.R. part 300, App. C, para. 36(a).

7. 34 C.F.R. part 300, App. C, para. 36(b).

8. 20 U.S.C. §1401(a)(20)(B).

9. 34 C.F.R. part 300, App. C, paras. 36(c), 38.

10. 34 C.F.R. part 300, App. C, paras. 38-39.

11. 34 C.F.R. part 300, App. C, para. 37.

12. 20 U.S.C. §1401(a)(20)(F).

13. 20 U.S.C. §§1401(a)(20)(C) and (E).

14. *Id.*

15. Georgia Association of Retarded Citizens v. McDaniel, 716 F.2d 1565 (11th Cir. 1983), *modified in part*, 740 F.2d 902 (1984), *cert. denied*, 469 U.S. 1228 (1985); Crawford v. Pittman, 708 F.2d 1028 (5th Cir. 1983); Battle v. Commonwealth of Pennsylvania, 629 F.2d 269 (3rd Cir. 1980), *cert. denied*, 452 U.S. 968 (1981). These cases also discuss the circumstances under which IDEA entitles children with disabilities to extended year services. For additional Court of Appeals opinions on this point, see Johnson v. Independent School District No. 4, 921 F.2d 1022 (10th Cir. 1990), *cert. denied*, 59 U.S.L.W. 3741 (1991); Cordrey v. Euckert, 917 F.2d 1460 (6th Cir. 1990), *cert. denied*, 111 S. Ct. 1391 (1991); Alamo Heights Independent School Board v. State Board of Education, 790 F.2d 1153 (5th Cir. 1986). Section 504 requirements regarding comparable benefits and services (for students with disabilities in comparison to non-disabled students) also apply to decisions regarding length of school day and year. See the discussion in Chapter II(A)(2), *supra*.

16. 20 U.S.C. §1401(a)(20)(C); 34 C.F.R. part 300, App. C, paras. 48, 52.

17. 20 U.S.C. §1401(a)(20)(D).

18. 20 U.S.C. §1401(a)(19).

19. *Id.*

20. 20 U.S.C. §1401(a)(20)(D).

21. 20 U.S.C. §1401(a)(20)(F). Proposed regulations published in the August 19, 1991 Federal Register would require that for all students aged sixteen and older, and for younger students whose need for transition services is being considered, the meeting also include a member of the public agency responsible for providing or supervising the transition services and, if appropriate, a representative of each other agency providing transition services included in the student's IEP. See 56 Fed. Reg. 41273 (1991).

22. 20 U.S.C. §1401(a)(20); 34 C.F.R. §§300.343(a) and 300.344(a).

23. 34 C.F.R. part 300, App. C, para. 13.

24. 20 U.S.C. §1401(a)(20); 34 C.F.R. §300.344(a)(4).

25. 34 C.F.R. §300.344(b).

26. 34 C.F.R. §300.344(a)(5). School districts may neither limit the number of individuals a parent may invite to a meeting nor require parents to provide prior notice of who they have chosen to invite. Inquiry of Marshall, EHLR 211:266 (4/28/81).

27. 20 U.S.C. §1401(a)(20) (defining "IEP," in part, as a document developed *in a meeting* by certain school personnel and parents) (emphasis added); 34 C.F.R. part 300, App. C, para. 55; Inquiry of Hellmuth, 16 EHLR [Education for the Handicapped Law Report] 503 (OSEP 1/30/90).

28. V.W. v. Favolise, 131 F.R.D. 654, 659 (D. Conn. 1990).

29. 34 C.F.R. §§300.343 and 300.345(a).

30. 34 C.F.R. §300.345(a).

31. 34 C.F.R. §300.345(c).

32. 34 C.F.R. §300.345(d).

33. *Id.*

34. E.H. v. Tirozzi, 735 F. Supp. 53 (D. Conn. 1990); *V.W. v. Favolise*, 131 F.R.D. at 659.

35. Rothschild v. Grottenthaler, 907 F.2d 286 (2nd Cir. 1990) (school district must provide parents with sign language interpreter for school-initiated meetings concerning academic or disciplinary progress of their children). OCR has gone farther than the *Rothschild* court, requiring interpreters at school system expense for PTA meetings, graduation ceremonies, "open house" programs, school plays and other non-academic programs. *See* Chicago (IL) Public Schools, District #299, 16 EHLR 1089 (OCR 4/25/90); Ramapo (NY) Central School District, 16 EHLR 559 (OCR 11/29/89); Inquiry of Parkin, EHLR 305:48 (OCR 6/11/88); *see also* OCR Staff Memorandum from William L. Smith, Acting Assistant Secretary for Civil Rights, dated December 20, 1989, published at 16 EHLR 542.

36. 34 C.F.R. §300.552(a)(2).

37. Spielberg v. Henrico County Public Schools, 853 F.2d 256, 259 (4th Cir. 1988); 34 C.F.R. §300.552(a)(2); 34 C.F.R. part 300, App. C, para. 5.

38. *Spielberg*, 853 F.2d at 259; *see also* Wetzel County (WV) Public School, EHLR 353:261 (OCR 5/17/89) (school violated §504 by adjusting goals and objectives so that they could be met in a particular classroom); *cf.* Todd D. v. Andrews, 933 F.2d 1576, 1580-81 (11th Cir. 1991) (district court erred by ordering alteration in IEP goals so that IEP could be implemented at existing placement, rather than ordering school system to provide placement capable of implementing IEP as written).

39. 34 C.F.R. §300.552.

40. 20 U.S.C. §1414(a)(5); 34 C.F.R. §300.343(d).

41. 34 C.F.R. part 300, App. C, paras. 10, 34.

42. 20 U.S.C. §1414(a)(5); 34 C.F.R. §300.343(d).

43. 34 C.F.R. §300.344(a).

44. 34 C.F.R. §300.343(a); 34 C.F.R. part 300, App. C, paras. 43, 51.

45. 34 C.F.R. §300.504(a).

46. See 34 C.F.R. §300.505.

47. 34 C.F.R. §300.504(a).

48. 34 C.F.R. part 300, App. C, para. 34.

VI.
Procedural Safeguards and Dispute Resolution Under IDEA and §504

IDEA contains an elaborate scheme of procedural safeguards designed to ensure that parents are involved in decisions affecting their child's education and, that when disputes develop nonetheless, they can challenge school system decisions.[1] The Supreme Court has stressed that these procedural requirements are not mere technicalities but, rather, the primary mechanism through which IDEA seeks to guarantee that the somewhat vaguely defined "appropriate" education it promises is actually delivered.[2]

While less specific than IDEA, the regulations implementing §504 also require entities operating public school programs to establish and implement a system of procedural safeguards meeting certain criteria.[3] Compliance with IDEA procedural safeguards is one way of meeting this §504 obligation.[4]

A. Surrogate Parents

Consistent with its emphasis on parent participation in IEP development and, as described below, advocacy by parents to ensure that children with disabilities receive the education to which they are entitled, IDEA requires states to ensure that all children with disabilities have the equivalent of a parent to act on their behalf. If a child's parents or guardian are not known or their whereabouts cannot be discovered after reasonable efforts, or if a child is a ward of the state, a "surrogate parent" must be appointed to fulfill the role otherwise played by parents under IDEA.[5] The surrogate parent cannot be an employee of a public agency involved in the education or care of the child,[6] must have no interest that conflicts with the child's interest,[7] and must have the knowledge and skills necessary to ensure that the child will be adequately represented.[8]

Once appointed a surrogate parent may — and has a duty to — represent the child in all matters relating to the child's identification, evaluation, IEP, placement and right to a free appropriate public education.[9]

B. Right to Prior Written Notice of School Decisions

Under IDEA, parents must be given prior written notice *any time* a school system proposes or refuses (usually in response to a parent's request) to initiate or change the identification, evaluation or educational placement of a child with disabilities or the provision of a free appropriate public education to the child.[10] Section 504 also requires notice of actions regarding the identification, evaluation or educational placement of students with disabilities.[11]

The notice required by IDEA must include:

- a description of the action proposed or refused by the school system;
- an explanation of why the school system proposes or refuses to take the action;
- a description of alternatives the school system considered along with an explanation of why those alternatives were rejected;
- a description of each evaluation procedure, test, record or report the school system used as a basis for its proposal or refusal; and
- a full explanation of all of the procedural safeguards available to parents under IDEA, including, among others, notice and consent rights, access to records, the right to an independent educational evaluation, due process hearing and appeal rights, and the right to bring a civil action in court.[12]

In addition, the notice must be written in language that the general public can understand and provided in the language or other mode of communication used by the parent.[13] If the parent's native language or other mode of communication is not a written one, the school system must ensure that the notice is translated, the parent understands it and that there is written evidence that these two requirements have been met.[14]

Unfortunately, these notice provisions are probably among the most often violated IDEA requirements. Notice meeting IDEA criteria, however, can be of enormous value to parents and their advocates in enforcing education rights. Advocates challenging school system decisions should consider making a demand for the required notice as a matter of course.

C. Access to Educational Records

Both IDEA and the §504 regulations guarantee parents the right to inspect and review educational records concerning their children.[15] School systems must honor requests to review records without unnecessary delay and before any IEP meeting or hearing.[16] In no event can a system take more than 45 days to comply.[17]

For purposes of IDEA, "record" means any information recorded in any way and includes tape and film.[18] IDEA access rights include the rights to:

- receive a response from school officials to reasonable requests for explanations and interpretations of the records;
- have a representative of the parent inspect and review the records; and
- obtain copies of records.[19]

The §504 regulations do not define "record" and do not detail the scope of access rights. However, compliance with IDEA access requirements will fulfill §504 requirements.[20] In addition, all students with disabilities and their parents are afforded access rights similar — and supplementary — to IDEA and §504 rights by the Family Educational Rights and Privacy Act ("FERPA")[21] and its implementing regulations.[22]

D. Administrative Complaints Under §504 and EDGAR

As explained in the following section, parents have the right to request an administrative due process hearing in order to vindicate IDEA and §504 rights as well as the right to bring an action in court. Parents may also file administrative complaints regarding IDEA and §504 violations with their state department of education (in regard to IDEA and/or §504) or the U.S. Department of Education Office of Civil Rights ("OCR") (in regard to §504). Complaints of this sort do *not* trigger a due process hearing; rather, they are "investigated" by the responsible agency, which then makes a determination as to whether rights have been violated.

1. Complaints to OCR Under §504

OCR is responsible for §504 enforcement. Any person who believes a school system has discriminated against a student in violation of §504 may file a written complaint.[23] Ordinarily, a complaint must be filed within 180 days of the date that the §504 violation occurred.[24] Complaints may be filed with the appropriate OCR regional office.[25]

OCR will investigate the complaint and, if it finds a violation, attempt to resolve the matter through informal means and obtain voluntary compliance from the offending school district.[26] Where informal resolution is not possible, OCR has the authority to terminate federal funding and take other legal action.[27] As a practical matter, however, OCR resolves most complaints without resort to such remedies.

Department of Education regulations expressly forbid school systems from intimidating, threatening, coercing, discriminating against or otherwise retaliating against anyone who has filed a §504 complaint or cooperated with a complaint investigation.[28] These regulations also generally prohibit retaliation against students and parents and others for engaging in activities protected by §504.[29]

2. EDGAR Complaints to a State Education Agency

States receiving grants through the U.S. Department of Education, including funds granted pursuant to IDEA, must comply with the Education Department General Administrative Regulations, or "EDGAR" regulations.[30] The EDGAR regulations require states to adopt written procedures for receiving and resolving complaints alleging that either the state itself or a subgrantee (such as a local school district) is violating a federal statute (such as IDEA or §504) or regulation governing a federally-funded program.[31]

In most states, the state department of education or other state education agency is responsible for receiving, investigating and resolving EDGAR complaints. Although the details may vary from state to state, complaint procedures must meet certain minimum criteria. They must provide for independent, on-site investigations when the state believes necessary.[32] In addition, complaints must be investigated, including any necessary independent, on-site investigation, and resolved within sixty calendar days of receipt; extensions may be granted only under exceptional circumstances.[33]

Any organization or individual may file a written EDGAR complaint,[34] and may request that the U.S. Secretary of Education review the state's final decision.[35] All states should have an EDGAR complaint mechanism in place.[36]

3. Advocacy Considerations

Depending upon the particular violation and other strategic concerns, advocates might file administrative complaints before, in conjunction with, or instead of invoking due process hearing procedures. In making these decisions, advocates and their clients should consider factors such as the following:

* whether even a favorable decision on an administrative complaint can provide all of the relief that may be available for the violation in question, including the individual compensatory relief available through due process;
* whether even a favorable decision on an individual complaint can provide all of the systemic relief that may be available for the violation in question;
* whether the legal principles involved are straightforward ones fairly obvious from the statute, regulations, or generally understood judicial decisions, or whether they are based on a more complicated analysis of statutes, regulations and case law;
* the extent to which the dispute revolves around factual disagreements, and so will require fact-finding by the complaint investigator;
* in regard to EDGAR complaints, their state agency's "track record" on IDEA and §504 enforcement;
* in regard to §504, the extent to which the OCR Regional Office has found and sought to remedy §504 violations in similar cases (advocates can determine the "track record" of their OCR region by making a Freedom of Information Act request for all documents relating to similar, past investigations); and
* the financial cost of a due process hearing compared to an EDGAR or OCR complaint.

Although an unfavorable administrative complaint decision is not binding in a subsequent due process hearing or civil action, advocates should also assess the extent to which an unfavorable decision might adversely influence any subsequent proceedings.

Finally, and as discussed in detail in section VI(F)(2), below, parents and students ordinarily must exhaust administrative remedies before taking special education matters to court. Filing an EDGAR or OCR complaint does *not* fulfill exhaustion requirements; before filing an action in court under IDEA and state law, parents and students ordinarily must go through due process hearings even if they have already gone through the administrative complaint process.[37] Again depending upon the nature of the violation, the client's goals and the importance of time, this may or may not be a significant consideration.

E. Due Process Hearings and Reviews

IDEA entitles parents and students to an impartial due process hearing on any matter related to the provision of a free appropriate public education including — but not limited to — identification, evaluation, and placement issues.[38] School districts, too, may initiate hearings.[39] Regardless of who requests the hearing, the educational agency must inform the parent of any free or low-cost legal and other relevant services available in the area.[40] Parents must also be provided this information upon request, even where no hearing is pending.[41]

The §504 regulations also require entities operating public school programs to establish an impartial administrative hearing and review system to address the complaints of students with disabilities.[42] Although the regulations do not set out specific criteria that hearing procedures must meet, they do provide that procedures meeting IDEA criteria will fulfill the §504 requirement as well.[43] Most states have a single hearing system for IDEA and §504 matters.

1. Single Versus Two Tiered Hearing/Review Systems

IDEA gives states two options for due process hearing systems. Under the first, due process hearings are conducted by the local school district.[44] Any party aggrieved by the decision can appeal to the state educational agency, which must conduct an impartial review of the hearing and make an independent decision on the case.[45] The official conducting the review must examine the entire record of the due process hearing; ensure that hearing procedures were consistent with due process; give the parties an opportunity for written and/or oral argument; seek additional evidence if necessary; and issue written findings and a written decision.[46]

If the reviewing officer seeks additional evidence, the hearing rights described below apply.[47] The decision of the reviewing official is final and binding unless appealed to a court.[48]

Under the second permissible system, due process hearings are conducted by the state educational agency.[49] Where this is the case, the hearing officer's decision *must* be final and binding (subject to the right to bring an action in court), and *cannot* be subject to any form of administrative review.[50]

2. Rights at Hearings

Regardless of whether the hearing is conducted at the local level or at the state level, the hearing officer cannot be an employee of an educational agency or unit involved in the education or care of the child.[51] Anyone with a personal or professional interest that would undermine his or her objectivity is likewise disqualified from serving.[52]

In addition to the right to an impartial hearing officer, parties to due process hearings have the following rights:

- the right to be represented by an attorney;
- the right to be accompanied and advised by individuals with special knowledge or training in the needs of children with disabilities;
- the right to present evidence;
- the right to confront and cross-examine witnesses;
- the right to compel the attendance of witnesses;
- the right to a written transcript or verbatim recording of the hearing; and
- the right to written findings of fact and written decisions.[53]

Either party may prohibit the other from presenting evidence it did not disclose at least five days before the hearing.[54] Parents but not other parties have the right to have the child present at the hearing and to open the hearing to the public.[55]

3. Timelines and Complaint Mediation

The IDEA regulations provide that a final decision in an impartial due process hearing must be rendered no later than 45 days after the hearing request is received.[56] In states that have opted for the local hearing/state-level review system, review decisions must be rendered no later than 30 days after the request for review is received.[57] Hearing and reviewing officers, however, may extend these deadlines at the request of either party.[58]

Although neither IDEA nor its regulations provide for mediation of special education disputes, many state schemes allow for complaint mediation prior to a due process hearing. While mediation is permissible and may be useful in some situations, it must be voluntary and cannot be used to deny or delay a parent's right to a due process hearing.[59] Mandatory mediation violates §504 as well.[60]

4. Advocacy Considerations

IDEA sets forth the minimum criteria state due process hearing schemes must meet. Most states have statutes or regulations that also address these issues. Advocates should check state law for additional requirements governing hearing procedures, rights and logistics.

In preparing for a hearing, it is crucial to plan for the possibility that the dispute might ultimately become the subject of an action in court. Should this occur, the rule requiring exhaustion of administrative remedies (discussed in further detail below) may prevent parties from raising issues they did not raise at the due process hearing.[61] Advocates should thus be careful to raise all issues and claims at the hearing, or risk "losing" them forever.

The same risk exists in regard to testimony and other evidence. As discussed below, some courts have held that there is only a *limited* right to introduce new evidence when an IDEA case reaches court. Under this view, under certain circumstances failure to present certain witnesses (or their complete testimony) or other evidence at the due process hearing means that they cannot be presented in court.[62] Thus ordinarily all relevant testimony and evidence should be presented at the hearing, and none "saved" for trial.

Advocates should also be aware that courts are required to give "due weight" to due process hearing outcomes under IDEA.[63] In addition, the party challenging the due process decision in court will have the burden of proving that the decision was wrong.[64] These factors underscore the importance of planning for due process hearings with court in mind.

F. Civil Action in Court

IDEA provides that any party aggrieved by a due process hearing decision (or, in states with a local hearing/state review system, the review decision) may bring a civil action in state or federal district court.[65] The court must receive the records of the administrative proceedings, hear additional evidence at the request of a party and base its decision on the preponderance of the evidence.[66] Courts must give "due weight...to...[state administrative] proceedings."[67] Where IDEA violations are found, courts may grant such relief as they deem appropriate.[68]

Section 504 does not expressly state that private individuals may sue in court for §504 violations. However, courts have generally held that they may bring a civil action to enforce §504, finding an implied right of action.[69]

Congress has expressly abrogated the states' Eleventh Amendment immunity from suit in federal court for violations of both IDEA[70] and §504,[71] effectively reversing two earlier Supreme Court decisions holding states immune.[72]

1. Statute of Limitations/Time Within Which to Sue

IDEA does not specify the time within which an aggrieved party must file suit. Courts must therefore "borrow" the statute of limitations for the most closely analogous state law claim, provided that it is consistent with the intent of IDEA.[73] The statute of limitations for bringing §504 claims in court is also "borrowed" from state law.[74]

Application of this rule in IDEA cases has resulted in statutes of limitations that vary widely from state to state.[75] And even *within* a state, statutes of limitations may vary depending upon the particular IDEA claim.[76] Some courts have adopted limitation periods as short as 30[77] or 60[78] days and 4 months.[79] It is important for non-attorney advocates to advise their clients to seek the advice of an attorney as soon as possible after an unfavorable due process hearing or review decision is issued.

2. Exhaustion of Administrative Remedies

IDEA   IDEA provisions regarding civil actions and jurisdiction ordinarily prohibit parents from bringing IDEA claims to court without first exhausting administrative remedies.[80] Although exhaustion may be excused if resort to administrative remedies would be "futile or inadequate,"[81] courts treat the requirement as a jurisdictional matter and usually read these exceptions narrowly.

The exhaustion requirement applies to particular *issues* as well as to the matter as a whole.[82] Filing an administrative complaint, such as an EDGAR complaint, does not constitute "exhaustion"; parents must go through due process hearings (and, in states with a local hearing/state review system, the review phase) in order to fulfill this requirement.[83]

§504 Ordinarily, individuals enforcing §504 rights are not required to exhaust administrative remedies before going to court.[84] However, parents and students with *§504* claims regarding public elementary or secondary education must exhaust *IDEA* administrative remedies before suing under certain circumstances. If the §504 action seeks relief that is also available under IDEA, the plaintiffs must fulfill IDEA exhaustion requirements *even if they had not intended to raise IDEA claims in court.*[85]

3. Additional Testimony and Evidence

Although IDEA provides that reviewing courts "shall hear additional evidence at the request of a party,"[86] the right to introduce new evidence may be a limited one. In *Town of Burlington v. Department of Education*,[87] the First Circuit Court of Appeals ruled that "additional" evidence means "supplemental" evidence, and that valid reasons for supplementing the administrative record will vary from case to case.[88] The court also held that witnesses cannot be presented in court simply to "repeat or embellish" their administrative hearing testimony.[89]

While refusing to prohibit anyone who testified or could have testified at the due process hearing from testifying in court, *Town of Burlington* did hold that such a witness is "rebuttably presumed" to be barred from testifying at trial.[90] In deciding whether to allow a hearing witness to testify despite this presumption, the court ruled, courts should "weigh heavily the important concerns of not allowing a party to undercut the statutory role of administrative expertise, the unfairness involved in one party's reserving its best evidence for trial, the reason the witness did not testify at the administrative hearing, and the conservation of judicial resources."[91]

G. Child's Status Pending Administrative and Judicial Proceedings

While due process or judicial proceedings are pending, the child is to remain in his or her then current educational placement unless the state or local education agency and his or her parents agree upon some other arrangement.[92] This IDEA provision is often referred to as the "stay put" or "status quo" provision, and has been characterized as "unequivocal" by the Supreme Court.[93] Stay-put rights apply to all changes in placement, including graduation[94] and changes related to school disciplinary action.[95]

Several courts have held that where a parent challenges a school system's placement proposal and prevails at the due process hearing level (or, where relevant, the state-level review), the decision is an "agreement" between parents and the state educational agency within the meaning of the stay-put provision.[96] Under this view, the placement can — and should — be implemented at public expense *even if the school system appeals the hearing or review decision in court.*

The stay-put provision prohibits *school systems* from unilaterally changing a student's placement pending due process and judicial proceedings. As explained below, *parents* with the resources to do so may change the child's placement at their own expense and, if they succeed in establishing that their placement is "appropriate" within the meaning of IDEA and the school system's proposed placement is not, be reimbursed by the school system.[97]

H. Remedies

IDEA permits courts to order such relief as is "appropriate" in special education cases.[98] Similarly, §504 entitles students who successfully pursue their rights under this statute to a variety of remedies as relief for having suffered discrimination. Due process hearing officers and courts can order a school system to take any number of actions in order to correct violations of IDEA and §504, including modifying an IEP, implementing an existing IEP it has failed to carry out, providing a particular placement, providing a particular related service(s), etc. Complaints to OCR can result in similar relief. In addition, compensatory education and reimbursement for special education and related services paid for by parents are available remedies under proper circumstances. Damages may also be available in IDEA and/or §504 cases.

1. Reimbursement

The Supreme Court approved retroactive reimbursement as an IDEA remedy in *School Committee of the Town of Burlington v. Department of Education.*[99] In that case, the court ruled that "appropriate" relief under IDEA can include an order requiring a local school district to reimburse parents for the cost of obtaining an appropriate education when the school system has failed to provide one.[100] School systems should ordinarily be ordered to reimburse parents for such costs unless "equitable considerations" would make such an order unfair under the circumstances of the case.[101]

Under *Burlington* retroactive reimbursement for private school tuition, for example, may be available where a hearing officer or a court determines that a school district failed to provide or offer the free appropriate public education required by IDEA, and that the private education obtained by parents was "appropriate."[102] Parents may also obtain reimbursement under IDEA for related services a school district should have but did not provide.[103] Transportation (including compensation for the expenditure of time and effort in providing transportation as well as out-of-pocket expenses),[104] summer programming[105] and tutoring,[106] as well as interest on loans obtained to finance educational costs,[107] have all been ordered reimbursed. Parents need not precisely replicate the placement a school district should have provided; parents may receive reimbursement for the costs incurred in providing special education or related services so long as these educational services meet the standard of "appropriateness" established by IDEA.[108]

Parents who win their IDEA case at the due process hearing level do not have to go to court to obtain an order requiring reimbursement; IDEA grants hearing officers the authority to order this remedy, and states must permit them to do so.[109]

Although most court cases seeking reimbursement have been decided under IDEA, reimbursement is available for §504 violations as well; a number of OCR complaint investigations have resulted in reimbursement by offending school districts.[110]

2. Compensatory Education

Since the Supreme Court's decision in *Burlington*, courts have consistently held that compensatory education, meaning additional educational and/or related services to make up for the time during which a school system failed to provide a free appropriate public education, is also an appropriate remedy under IDEA.[111] Comparing compensatory education to the reimbursement approved in *Burlington*, these courts have recognized that without compensatory education, students whose parents lack the resources to place them in private programs and seek reimbursement have no way to vindicate their IDEA rights.[112] Compensatory education should therefore be available whenever necessary to secure the right to a free appropriate public education. IDEA grants due process hearing officers the authority to award compensatory education.[113] Parents should not have to go to court simply to secure this particular remedy.

Depending upon the circumstances, the particular IDEA violation and the student's needs, compensatory education may take the form of additional special education or related services during the school day, after usual school hours, or during the summer or other vacation periods. It may also take the form of additional *years* of special education and related services, requiring school systems to continue educational services beyond the age at which a student's entitlement to public education would otherwise end — including education beyond age 21.[114]

As is the case with reimbursement, most reported judicial decisions awarding compensatory education have done so under IDEA, with no discussion of §504.[115] Resolutions of OCR complaints, however, have resulted in the provision of compensatory education — including education beyond age 21 — to remedy §504 violations in a number of cases.[116]

3. Damages

Courts have not yet definitively addressed the issue of whether damages (other than reimbursement or compensatory education) are available for violations of IDEA rights. While some courts have stated that IDEA does not authorize damages in any circumstances,[117] others have left open the possibility of damages under "exceptional" or "egregious" circumstances.[118]

Even if damages are not available under IDEA in and of itself, damages should be available if IDEA is linked with 42 U.S.C. §1983, which allows an individual who has been deprived of rights granted by a federal statute to bring an action for damages under certain circumstances. Prior to 1986 a number of judicial decisions, including the Supreme Court's decision in *Smith v. Robinson*,[119] held or suggested that a §1983 action could not be brought to vindicate the substantive IDEA right to a free appropriate public education.[120]

This is no longer the case, however. The Handicapped Children's Protection Act of 1986 ("HCPA")[121] expressly provides that IDEA does not limit the rights or remedies available under the Constitution, §504 or other federal statutes protecting the rights of children and youth with disabilities.[122] The legislative history of the HCPA demonstrates that this provision includes §1983.[123] There thus should be no question that a §1983 action can be brought to redress IDEA violations. It should also be possible to bring a damage claim for violation of §504 rights by linking §1983 with particular §504 regulations. Damages may also be available under §504 directly, independently of §1983; this issue has yet to be addressed by the courts.[124]

I. Availability of Attorneys Fees

The HCPA also amended IDEA to provide for attorneys fees. Parents who prevail in IDEA disputes may now recover reasonable fees and costs, subject to certain conditions.[125]

Fees and costs may *not* be awarded for services performed after a written settlement offer is made to the parents if:

the offer was made more than 10 days before the start of the due process hearing or, in the case of court proceedings, within the time specified by Rule 68 of the Federal Rules of Civil Procedure (currently more than 10 days before trial starts)

AND

the offer is not accepted within 10 days

AND

the court or administrative officer finds that the relief finally obtained by the parents is not more favorable than the settlement offer, unless the parent was substantially justified in rejecting the offer.[126]

Attorneys fees are available for parents who prevail in administrative due process proceedings (with no subsequent appeal to court), as well as for those who prevail in court.[127] Fees are also recoverable for work done in settling IDEA disputes prior to a due process hearing.[128]

Apart from IDEA provisions regarding attorneys fees, parties who prevail on §504 claims in court may be awarded attorneys fees under §504.[129]

Notes

1. Procedural safeguards are set out in 20 U.S.C. §1415.

2. Board of Education of the Hendrick Hudson Central School District v. Rowley, 458 U.S. 176, 205-06, 102 S. Ct. 3034, 3050-51 (1982).

3. 34 C.F.R. §104.36.

4. *Id.*

5. 20 U.S.C. §1415(b)(1)(B); 34 C.F.R. §300.514.

6. 20 U.S.C. §1415(b)(1)(B); 34 C.F.R. § 300.514(d)(1).

7. 34 C.F.R. §300.514(c)(2)(i).

8. *Id.*

9. 34 C.F.R. §§300.514(e); *see also* 34 C.F.R. part 300, App. C, para. 27.

10. 20 U.S.C. §1415(b)(1)(C); 34 C.F.R. §300.504(a).

11. 34 C.F.R. §104.36.

12. 34 C.F.R. §300.505(a).

13. 20 U.S.C. §1415(b)(1)(D);34 C.F.R. §300.505(b).

14. 34 C.F.R. §300.505(c).

15. 20 U.S.C. §1415(b)(1)(A); 34 C.F.R. §§300.502 and 300.562-300.569; 34 C.F.R. §104.36.

16. 34 C.F.R. §300.562(a).

17. *Id.*

18. 34 C.F.R. 99.3, incorporated into the IDEA regulations by reference by 34 C.F.R. §300.560.

19. 34 C.F.R. §300.562.

20. 34 C.F.R. §104.36.

21. 20 U.S.C. §1232g, also known as the Buckley Amendment.

22. 34 C.F.R. §99.1 *et seq.* In regard to inspection and review of records by parents and students, see §§99.10 through 99.12.

23. 34 C.F.R. §100.7(b). 34 C.F.R. §104.61 makes 34 C.F.R. §§100.6-100.10 applicable to §504 violations.

24. 34 C.F.R. §100.7(b).

25. The addresses of OCR regional offices are listed in Appendix B. Although §504 complaints are investigated by the appropriate regional office, OCR has ruled that the decisions of one regional office are binding on other regions. *See* Inquiry by Rhys, EHLR 305:26 (OCR 4/14/85).

26. 34 C.F.R. §100.7(c) and (d).

27. 34 C.F.R. §100.8(a).

28. 34 C.F.R. §100.7(e).

29. *Id. See, e.g.*, Auburn (AL) City School District, EHLR 353:374 (OCR 8/7/89) (school district reversal of prior eligibility determination was, under the circumstances, illegal retaliation against parent and student for parent's participation in meetings and filing of complaints with OCR and state department of education); Frederick County (MD) School District, EHLR 352:407 (OCR 3/25/87) (treating complainant's requests for records differently than all others constituted retaliation for her protected advocacy activities on behalf of her sons and others); Bethpage (NY) Union Free School District, EHLR 353:147 (OCR 1988) [Complaint No. 02-88-1010] (under the circumstances, referring parent to Child Protective Services for educational neglect constituted impermissible retaliation for exercise of §504 rights).

30. 34 C.F.R. §76.1 *et seq.*

31. 34 C.F.R. §76.780(a).

32. 34 C.F.R. §76.780(a)(3).

33. 34 C.F.R. §76.781(a) and (b).

34. 34 C.F.R. §76.782.

35. 34 C.F.R. §76.781(c).

36. On August 19, 1991 the Department of Education published proposed IDEA regulations that would significantly change procedures for complaints regarding IDEA violations. See 56 Fed. Reg. 41275. The proposal substitutes an IDEA-specific complaint system for the EDGAR regulations currently applicable. The proposed regulations parallel EDGAR requirements regarding on-site investigations, the 60-day time frame for resolving complaints and the right to request review by the U.S. Secretary of Education. In addition, however, they would require the state department of education (or other designated state education agency) to adopt procedures for informing parents and other interested individuals about complaint procedures; to give a complaining party the opportunity to submit additional information (beyond the initial written complaint), either orally or in writing, about the alleged IDEA violation; to issue a written decision that addresses each allegation in the complaint and contains findings of fact, conclusions, and an explanation of the rationale underlying the final decision; and to develop procedures for meaningful implementation of decisions on complaints, including technical assistance, negotiation and corrective action to see that offending school systems comply.

37. *See* Christopher W. v. Portsmouth School Committee, 877 F.2d 1089, 1095 and n.4 (1st Cir. 1989).

38. 20 U.S.C. §§1415(b)(1)(E) and (b)(2).

39. 34 C.F.R. §300.506(a).

40. 34 C.F.R. §300.506(c).

41. *Id.*

42. 34 C.F.R. §104.36.

43. *Id.*

44. 20 U.S.C. §1415(b)(2).

45. 20 U.S.C. §1415(c).

46. 34 C.F.R. §300.510(b).

47. *See* 34 C.F.R. §§300.510(b)(3) and 300.508.

48. 20 U.S.C. 1415(e)(1).

49. 20 U.S.C. §1415(b)(2).

50. 20 U.S.C. §§1415(c), 1415(e)(2). *See also, e.g.,* Muth v. Smith, 646 F. Supp. 280, 283-286 (E.D. Pa. 1986), *a'ffd. on other grounds sub nom.* Muth v. Central Bucks School District, 839 F.2d 113 (3rd Cir. 1988), *rev'd on other grounds sub nom.* Dellmuth v. Muth, 109 S.Ct. 2397 (1989); Diamond v. McKenzie, 602 F. Supp. 632, 638-639 (D.D.C. 1985); Monahan v. State of Nebraska, 491 F. Supp. 1074, 1086 (D. Neb. 1980), *aff'd in part, vacated in part on other grounds,* 645 F.2d 592 (8th Cir. 1981), *cert. denied,* 460 U.S. 1012 (1982).

51. 20 U.S.C. §1415(b)(2).

52. 34 C.F.R. §300.507(a)(2).

53. 20 U.S.C. §1415(d); 34 C.F.R. §300.508.

54. 34 C.F.R. §300.508(a)(3).

55. 34 C.F.R. §300.508(b).

56. 34 C.F.R. §300.512(a).

57. 34 C.F.R. §300.512(b).

58. 34 C.F.R. §300.512(c).

59. *See* Comment to 34 C.F.R. §300.506.

60. Bristol-Plymouth Regional Vocational-Technical School District, EHLR 353:241 (OCR 6/27/89) (mandatory 30 day mediation period violated 34 C.F.R. §104.36 by delaying parent's right to due process hearing immediately after rejection of IEP).

61. *See, e.g.,* Leonard v. McKenzie, 869 F.2d 1558, 1563 (D.C. Cir. 1989); Howell v. Waterford Public Schools, 731 F.Supp. 1314, 1315-1316 (E.D. Mich. 1990).

62. *See, e.g.,* Town of Burlington v. Department of Education, 736 F.2d 773, 790-791 (1st Cir. 1984), *aff'd. on other grounds,* 471 U.S. 359, 105 S. Ct. 1996 (1985); Anderson v. District of Columbia, 877 F.2d 1018, 1025 (D.C. Cir. 1989).

63. *Rowley,* 458 U.S. at 206, 102 S.Ct. at 3051; *see also Town of Burlington,* 736 F.2d at 791-792.

64. Roland M. v. Concord School Committee, 910 F.2d 983, 991 (1st Cir. 1990), *cert. denied,* 111 S. Ct. 1122 (1991).

65. 20 U.S.C. §1415(e)(2).

66. *Id.*

67. *Rowley*, 458 U.S. at 206, 102 S. Ct. at 3051. An examination of the standards of review that have evolved from this *Rowley* dictate is beyond the scope of this discussion. For examples of some of the ways in which courts have discussed standard of review issues in various factual and procedural contexts see, e.g., *Town of Burlington*, 736 F.2d at 790-91 (1st Cir.); Burke County Board of Education v. Denton, 895 F.2d 973 (4th Cir. 1990); Doe v. Smith, 879 F.2d 1340 (6th Cir. 1989), *cert. denied*, 110 S. Ct. 730 (1990); Lachman v. Illinois State Board of Education, 852 F.2d 290 (7th Cir. 1988), *cert. denied*, 109 S. Ct. 308; Gregory K. v. Longview School District, 811 F.2d 1307 (9th Cir. 1987); Johnson v. Independent School District No. 4, 921 F.2d 1022 (10th Cir. 1990), *cert. denied*, 59 U.S.L.W. 3741 (1991); Jefferson County Board of Education v. Breen, 853 F.2d 853 (11th Cir. 1988); Kerkam v. McKenzie, 862 F.2d 884 (D.C. Cir. 1988).

68. 20 U.S.C. §1415(e)(2).

69. *See, e.g.,* Leary v. Crapsey, 566 F.2d 863 (2nd Cir. 1977); N.A.A.C.P. v. Medical Center, 599 F.2d 1247 (3rd Cir. 1979); Meiner v. State of Missouri, 673 F.2d 969, 973 (8th Cir. 1982), *cert. denied*, 459 U.S. 909 (1982); Southeastern Community College v. Davis, 574 F.2d 1158 (4th Cir. 1978), *rev'd and remanded on other grounds*, 442 U.S. 397 (1979); University of Texas v. Camenisch, 616 F.2d 127 (5th Cir. 1980), *vacated and remanded on other grounds*, 451 U.S. 390 (1981); Jennings v. Alexander, 715 F.2d 1036 (6th Cir. 1983), *rev'd on other grounds sub nom Alexander v. Choate*, 469 U.S. 287 (1985); Lloyd v. Regional Transportation Authority, 548 F.2d 1277 (7th Cir 1977); United Handicapped Federation v. Andre, 558 F.2d 413 (8th Cir. 1977); Kling v. County of Los Angeles, 633 F.2d 876 (9th Cir. 1980); Pushkin v. Regents of University of Colorado, 658 F.2d 1372 (10th Cir. 1981); Jones v. M.A.R.T.A., 681 F.2d 1376 (11th Cir. 1982), *cert. denied*, 465 U.S. 1099 (1984). *See also* Consolidated Rail Corporation v. Darrone, 465 U.S. 624, 630 (1984) ("...§504 authorizes a plaintiff who alleges intentional discrimination to bring an equitable action for back pay").

70. See §103 of the Education of the Handicapped Act Amendments of 1990, Pub. L. 101-474, 104 Stat. 1106, codified at 20 U.S.C. §1403.

71. See §1003 of the Rehabilitation Act Amendments of 1986, 100 Stat. 1845, codified at 42 U.S.C. §2000d-7.

72. The two cases are Atascadero State Hospital v. Scanlon, 473 U.S. 234, 105 S. Ct. 3142 (1985) (regarding §504) and Dellmuth v. Muth, 491 U.S. 223, 109 S. Ct. 2397 (1989) (regarding IDEA).

73. Wilson v. Garcia, 471 U.S. 261, 266-67 (1984); Spiegler v. District of Columbia, 866 F.2d 461 (D.C. Cir. 1989); Tokarcik v. Forest Hills School District, 665 F. 2d 443 (3rd Cir. 1981), *cert. denied*, 458 U.S. 1121 (1982).

74. *See, e.g.,* Andrews v. Consolidated Rail Corporation, 831 F.2d 678 (7th Cir. 1987); Alexopulos v. San Francisco Unified School District, 817 F.2d 551 (9th Cir. 1987); Doe v. Southeastern University, 732 F. Supp 7 (D. D.C. 1990); Bush v. Commonwealth Edison Co., 732 F. Supp. 895 (N.D.Ill. 1990); Wallace v. Town of Stratford Board of Education, 674 F. Supp. 67 (D. Conn.

1986).

75. *Compare, e.g., Spiegler, supra,* (adopting 30 day statute of limitations) *with* Schimmel v. Spillane, 819 F.2d 477 (4th Cir. 1987) (rejecting 30 day period as contrary to policy underlying the IDEA and applying 1-year statute of limitations) *and Tokarcik, supra* (rejecting 30 days as contrary to IDEA policy and adopting 2-year limitations period).

76. *Compare, e.g.,* Janzen v. Knox County Board of Education, 790 F.2d. 484 (6th Cir. 1986) (Tennessee statute of limitations governing actions for reimbursement under IDEA is 3 year period applicable to actions for money owed for personal services rendered) *with* Doe v. Smith, 16 EHLR 65 (M.D. Tenn. 1988) (Tennessee statute of limitations applicable to non-reimbursement matters under IDEA is 60 days).

77. *Spiegler, supra* (District of Columbia).

78. *Doe v. Smith, supra* (for non-reimbursement cases in Tennessee).

79. Adler v. New York Department of Education, 760 F.2d 454 (2nd Cir. 1985) (New York); Thomas v. Staats, 633 F. Supp. 797 (S.D. W.Va. 1985) (120 days, West Virginia).

80. Honig v. Doe, 484 U.S. 305, 108 S.Ct. 592, 606 (1988).

81. *Id.*

82. *Leonard,* 869 F.2d at 1558; *Howell,* 731 F. Supp. at 1315-1316.

83. Christopher W., *supra.*

84. *See, e.g., Pushkin,* 658 F.2d at 1381; *Camenisch, supra*; Georgia State Conference of Branches of the N.A.A.C.P. v. State of Georgia, 775 F.2d 1403 (11th Cir. 1985); *Lloyd, supra*; *Meiner, supra*; New Mexico Association for Retarded Citizens v. State of New Mexico, 678 F.2d 847 (10th Cir. 1982); Mrs. W. v. Tirozzi, 832 F.2d 748 (2nd Cir. 1987).

85. 20 U.S.C. §1415(f). This provision was added to IDEA by the Handicapped Children's Protection Act of 1986, P.L. 99-372, 100 Stat. 796.

86. 20 U.S.C. §1415(e)(2).

87. 736 F.2d 773 (1st Cir 1984), *aff'd. on other grounds*, 471 U.S. 359 (1989).

88. *Town of Burlington,* 736 F.2d at 790. The court offered the following as examples of reasons for supplementation: gaps in the hearing transcript due to mechanical failure; unavailability of a witness; improper exclusion of evidence by the hearing or review officer; and evidence concerning relevant events occurring after the due process hearing. *Id.*

89. *Id.*

90. *Id.,* 736 F.2d at 790-791.

91. *Id.,* 736 F.2d at 791. For additional cases discussing the extent to which additional evidence may be presented at trial, see Roland M. v. Concord School Committee, 910 F.2d 983 (1st Cir. 1990), *cert. denied*, 111 S. Ct. 1122 (1991); Metropolitan Government of Nashville and Davidson County v. Cook, 915 F.2d 232, 234-35 (6th Cir. 1990) (refusing to adopt *Town of Burlington* limitations); Anderson v. District of Columbia, 877 F.2d 1018,

1025 (D.C. Cir. 1989) (admonishing attorney who called no witnesses at administrative hearing but presented two experts at trial for "treat[ing] the administrative proceedings as just an optional stop on the way to court"); Jean N. v. Tirozzi, 17 EHLR 580 (D. Conn. 1991); Barwacz v. Michigan Department of Education, 681 F. Supp. 427, 431-432 (W.D. Mich. 1988) (citing *Town of Burlington* and permitting student who did not testify at administrative hearing to testify in court).

92. 20 U.S.C. §1415(e)(3). The Court of Appeals for the D.C. Circuit has held that §1415(e)(3) applies only during the pendency of administrative due process and trial court level proceedings, and not pending further review by appellate courts. See Andersen v. District of Columbia, 877 F.2d 1018, 1093 (D.C. Cir. 1989).

93. *Honig*, 108 S. Ct. at 604. For a discussion of "stay put" rights in contexts other than due process and judicial review, see Chapter VIII, *infra*.

94. Cronin v. Board of East Ramapo Central School District, 689 F. Supp. 197 (S.D.N.Y. 1988); Stock v. Massachusetts Hospital School, 392 Mass. 705, 467 N.E.2d 448 (1984), *cert. denied*, 474 U.S. 844 (1985); Inquiry of Richards, 17 EHLR 288 (OSEP 1991).

95. Discipline issues are discussed below in Chapter VIII.

96. See Grace B. v. Lexington School Committee, 762 F. Supp. 416 (D. Mass 1991); Kantak v. Liverpool Central School District, 16 EHLR 643 (N.D.N.Y. 1990); Department of Education of Hawaii v. Mr. and Mrs. S., 632 F. Supp. 1268 (D. Hawaii 1986); Blazejewski v. Board of Education of Allegany Central School District, 560 F. Supp. 701 (W.D.N.Y. 1983).

97. Town of Burlington School Committee v. Department of Education, 471 U.S. 359, 105 S. Ct. 1996 (1985).

98. 20 U.S.C. §1415(e)(2). The statute does not define "appropriate."

99. 471 U.S. 359, 105 S. Ct. 1996 (1985).

100. 471 U.S. at 370, 105 S. Ct. at 2003. As previously noted, IDEA directs courts to "grant such relief as the court determines is appropriate," 20 U.S.C. §1415(e)(2), without defining or describing "appropriate" relief.

101. *See Town of Burlington*, 471 U.S. at 374, 105 S. Ct. at 2005. Parents and their advocates should be aware that reimbursement is not necessarily available in all cases. In *Town of Burlington*, the Supreme Court stated that courts may take "equitable considerations" into account in deciding whether to order reimbursement in a particular case and, if so, in what amount. *Id.* The lower court opinion in *Town of Burlington* stated that such considerations might include whether or not parents consulted the school district before placing their child in a private school, or whether parents attempted to reach an agreement or compromise before doing so. 736 F.2d at 799; see also 736 F.2d at 801-802 ("...whether to order reimbursement, and at what amount, is a question to be determined by balancing the equities...[f]actors that should be taken into account include the parties' compliance or noncompliance with state and federal regulations

pending review, the reasonableness of the parties' positions, and like matters"). Since *Town of Burlington*, some courts have held or suggested that reimbursement may be denied or reduced to parents who place their children privately without first investigating the school district's proposal, informing district officials that they are dissatisfied with the district program or proposal, asking the school district to fund the private placement and/or requesting a due process hearing on the issue. *See, e.g.*, Wexler v. Westfield Board of Education, 784 F. 2d 176 (3rd. Cir. 1986), *cert. denied*, 479 U.S. 825; Gillette v. Fairland Board of Education, 725 F. Supp 343 (S.D. Ohio 1989); B.G. v. Cranford Board of Education, 702 F. Supp. 1158 (D.N.J. 1988); Garland Independent School District v. Wilks, 657 F. Supp 1163 (N.D. Tex. 1987). Where such parental "missteps" are caused by school district violations of IDEA notice requirements, however, reimbursement rights should remain intact. Hall v. Vance, 774 F. 2d 629, 633-634, n.4 (4th Cir. 1985) (even if *Burlington* were limited to placements made during the pendency of review proceedings, "where failure to initiate review proceedings before changing a child's placement is the result of a school system's own failure to inform the parents of available avenues of review, the unilateral placement of the child should not, in our view, be treated as a waiver of a reimbursement remedy").

102. *Burlington*, 471 U.S. at 370, 105 S. Ct. at 2002-2003.

103. *See, e.g.*, Rapid City School District 51-4 v. Vahle, 733 F. Supp. 1364 (D.S.D. 1990), *aff'd.* 922 F.2d 476 (8th Cir. 1990).

104. Hurry v. Jones, 734 F.2d 879 (1st Cir. 1984); *see also* Alamo Heights Independent School District v. State Board of Education, 790 F.2d 1153 (5th Cir. 1986).

105. *Alamo Heights, supra.*

106. *Hall, supra.*

107. Board of Education of the County of Cabell v. Dienelt, 1986-87 EHLR DEC. 558:305 (S.D.W.V. 1987), *aff'd.*, 843 F. 2d 813 (4th Cir. 1988).

108. *See Alamo Heights*, 790 F.2d at 1153 (program in which parent enrolled child, "although it might not have been adequate under the EAHCA, was better than no summer program at all...*Burlington* rule is not so narrow as to permit reimbursement only when the interim placement chosen by the parent is found to be the exact proper placement required under the Act"); *see also* Garland Independent School District v. Wilks, 657 F. Supp. 1163, 1166-67 (N.D. Tex. 1987) (finding that a low income parent was entitled to reimbursement for furnishing those services intended, to the extent the parent could afford, to create a "facsimile" of the residential placement ultimately ordered by the court).

109. Inquiry of Van Buiten, EHLR 211:429A (Office of Special Education and Rehabilitative Services 6/17/87). *See also* S-1 v. Spangler, 650 F. Supp. 1427 (M.D.N.C. 1986), *vacated as moot*, 832 F.2d 294 (4th Cir. 1987).

110. *See, e.g.*, Northwest Jefferson County (MO) R-I School District, EHLR 257:354 (OCR 3/31/82); Fremont (CO) School District RE-3, EHLR 257:273 (OCR 10/27/80); Clark County (NV) School District, EHLR 257:245 (OCR 1/16/81); School District #220 (IL), EHLR 257:200 (OCR 2/12/81). *See also* Memorandum to Gary D. Jackson, Regional Civil Rights Director, Region X from William L. Smith, Acting Assistant Secretary for Civil Rights of June 28, 1989, reprinted at EHLR 307:10.

111. *See, e.g.*, Lester H. v. Gilhool, 916 F.2d 865 (3rd Cir. 1990), *cert. denied*, 111 S. Ct. 1317 (1991); Burr v. Sobol, 863 F.2d 1071 (2nd Cir. 1989), *vacated and remanded* 109 S. Ct. 3209 (1989), *on remand, aff'd. per curiam*, 888 F.2d 258 (2nd Cir. 1989), *cert. denied* 58 U.S.L.W. 3545 (2/27/90); Jefferson County Board of Education v. Breen, 853 F.2d 853 (11th Cir. 1988); Miener v. Missouri, 800 F.2d 749 (8th Cir. 1986); Max M. v. Thompson, 592 F. Supp. 1450 (N.D. Ill. 1984). *See also* Jackson v. Franklin County School Board, 806 F.2d 632,631 (5th Cir. 1986) (on remand "...the district court must determine what damages, either monetary, or in the form of remedial education services...would be appropriate at this time"); Campbell v. Talladega County Board of Education, 518 F. Supp. 47 (N.D. Ala. 1981).

112. *See, e.g.*, *Meiner*, 800 F.2d at 753; *Breen*, 853 F.2d at 857-58; *Burr*, 863 F.2d at 1078.

113. Inquiry of Kohn, 17 EHLR 522 (OSEP 2/13/91).

114. *See* Todd D. v. Andrews, 933 F. 2d 1576, 1584 (11th Cir. 1991); *Burr, supra; Breen, supra; Lester H., supra; Campbell, supra; Max M., supra; but see* Alexopulos v. Riles, 784 F.2d 1408 (9th Cir. 1986) (finding claim to be time-barred and beyond statutory cut-off intended by Congress); McDowell v. Fort Bend Independent School District, 737 F. Supp. 386 (S.D. Tex. 1990) (finding IDEA claim of 23 year-old student moot).

115. *Lester H., supra*, is one exception. While the Third Circuit's opinion discussed only IDEA, the district court opinion awarding compensatory education notes §504 as well as IDEA violations. *See* Lester H. v. Carroll, 16 EHLR 10 (E.D. Penn. 1989). The Second Circuit has explicitly recognized the availability of compensatory education under §504. *See* Mrs. C. v. Wheaton, 916 F.2d 69, 75-76 (2nd Cir. 1990).

116. *See, e.g.*, Augusta County (VA) School Division, EHLR 352:233 (OCR 8/21/86); Chicago (IL) Board of Education; EHLR 257:568 (OCR 7/9/84); Clermont (OH) Northeastern Schools, EHLR 257:577 (OCR 7/23/84); Kanawha County (WV) School District, EHLR 257:439 (OCR 9/28/83) (beyond age 21); Chicago (IL) Board of Education, EHLR 257:453 (OCR 3/11/83).

117. *See, e.g. Hall*, 774 F.2d at 633 n.3 (dictum); Anderson v. Thompson, 658 F.2d 1205, 1213-14 & n.12 (7th Cir. 1981); Waterman v. Marquette-Alger Intermediate School District, 739 F. Supp. 361, 364 (W.D. Mich. 1990); Barnett v. Fairfax County Board of Education, 721 F. Supp. 755, 756 (E.D. Va. 1989); Smith v. Philadelphia School District, 679 F. Supp. 479, 484 (E.D. Penn. 1988) (dictum); Silano v. Tirozzi, 651 F. Supp. 1021, 1027 (D.

Conn. 1987); Davis v. Maine Endwell Central School District, 542 F. Supp. 1257, 1261 (N.D.N.Y. 1982). See also Quackenbush v. Johnson City School District, 716 F.2d 141, 149 (2nd Cir. 1983), *cert. denied*, 465 U.S. 1071 (1984) (issue not reached); Miener v. Missouri, 673 F.2d 969, 979-980 (8th Cir. 1982), *cert. denied*, 459 U.S. 916 (there might be a right to damages in "exceptional circumstances"), subsequent decision, 800 F. 2d 749, 753-43, characterizing *Burlington* as having stated that in IDEA, Congress chose not to establish a general damages remedy.

118. *See* Manecke v. School Board of Pinellas County, 762 F.2d 912, 915-16 at n.2 (11th Cir. 1985), *cert. denied*, 474 U.S. 1062 (1986); Department of Education v. Katherine D., 727 F.2d 809, 816-17 (9th Cir. 1984), *cert. denied*, 471 U.S. 1117 (1985); Powell v. Defore, 699 F.2d 1078, 1081 (11th Cir. 1983); Marvin H. v. Austin Independent School District, 714 F.2d 1348, 1356 (5th Cir. 1983); Barwacz v. Michigan Department of Education, 674 F. Supp. 1296, 1307 (W.D. Mich. 1987); Geriasimou v. Ambach, 636 F. Supp. 1504, 1512 (E.D.N.Y. 1986); Hudson v. Wilson, 1986-87 EHLR DEC. 558:186, :190-91 (W.D. Va. 1986); *Campbell, supra*, 518 F. Supp. at 57; White v. California, 195 Cal. App. 3d 452 (1987); *see also Jackson* 806 F.2d at 631-32 (5th Cir. 1986) (remanding for a determination of damages, "either monetary or in the form of remedial education services," after holding that school officials had violated student's "due process rights, as contemplated by the Fourteenth Amendment and as specifically enumerated by the EHA...").

119. 468 U.S. 992, 104 S. Ct. 3457 (1984).

120. *Smith* held that where IDEA (then the EHA) is available to a child with disabilities "...asserting a right to a free appropriate public education, based either on the EHA or on the Equal Protection Clause of the Fourteenth Amendment, the EHA is the exclusive avenue through which the child and his parents or guardian can pursue their claim." 468 U.S. at 1013, 104 S. Ct. 3469. *Smith* further held that "...where...whatever remedy might be provided under § 504 is provided with more clarity and precision under the EHA, a plaintiff may not circumvent or enlarge on the remedies available under the EHA by resort to § 504." 468 U.S. at 1021, 104 S. Ct. at 3473. The Handicapped Children's Protection Act of 1986, Pub. L. 99-372, 100 Stat. 796., effectively reversed these holdings.

121. Pub. L. 99-372, 100 Stat. 796.

122. The pertinent HCPA provision is codified at 20 U.S.C. §1415(f).

123. *See* H.R. Conf. Rep. No. 687, 99th Cong., 2d Sess. 7, *reprinted in* 1986 U.S. Code Cong. & Ad. News 1807, 1809; see also H.R. Rep. 296, 99th Cong., 1st. sess., 3-7 (1985).

124. Whether damages are available for §504 violations without resort to §1983 is unclear. 29 U.S.C. §794a(a)(2) provides that "[t]he remedies, procedures and rights set forth in Title VI of the Civil Rights Act of 1964 [which bars discrimination on the basis of race, color or national origin in programs or activities receiving Federal financial assistance]...shall be

available to any person" aggrieved by violations of §504. The availability of §504 damages thus turns on the availability of damages for Title VI violations--a question that has not been definitively addressed by the courts and may vary from circuit to circuit. An analysis of the law of Title IV remedies is beyond the scope of this discussion. Advocates should be aware, however, that shortly before this writing the Supreme Court granted *certiorari* in Franklin v. Gwinnett County Public Schools, 911 F.2d 617 (11th Cir. 1990). See 59 U.S.L.W. 3823 (6/11/91). This case presents the issue of whether damages are available for violations of Title IX of the Education Amendments of 1972 which, like §504, incorporates Title VI remedies.

125. 20 U.S.C. §1415(e)(4).

126. 20 U.S.C. §1415(e)(4)(D) and (E).

127. Moore v. District of Columbia Board of Education, 907 F.2d 165 (D.C. Cir. 1990), *vacating* 886 F.2d. 335, *cert. denied*, 111 S. Ct. 556 (1990); McSomebodies v. Burlington Elementary and Secondary School District, 886 F.2d 1558 (9th Cir. 1989), *supplemented* March 2, 1990, 897 F.2d 974; Mitten v. Muscogee Cty. School District, 877 F.2d 932 (11th Cir. 1989), *cert. denied* 110 S.Ct. 1117 (1990); Duane M. v. Orleans Parish School Board, 861 F.2d 115 (5th Cir. 1988); Eggers v. Bullitt County School District, 854 F.2d 892 (6th Cir. 1988).

128. Shelly C. v. Venus Independent School District, 878 F.2d 862 (5th Cir. 1989), *cert. denied*, 110 S. Ct. 729 (1990); Abu-Sahyun v. Palo Alto Unified School District, 843 F.2d 1250 (9th Cir. 1988); Terefenko v. Stafford Township Board of Education, 17 EHLR 573 (D.N.J. 1991); Rossi v. Gosling, 696 F. Supp. 1079 (E.D. Va. 1988).

129. 29 U.S.C. §794a(b).

VII.
Discrimination Against Children Who Have AIDS, are HIV Positive or Are Carriers of Hepatitis B

Recent attempts to exclude children with AIDS from school, or to place students in overly restrictive educational settings simply because of their HIV status, follow earlier, ongoing, similar attempts to discriminate against children who are carriers of Hepatitis B. Section 504 protects children from such discrimination. Under certain circumstances, IDEA may also come into play.

A. Rights Under §504

As previously explained in Chapter I, §504 prohibits discrimination against "individual[s] with handicaps" who are "otherwise qualified" to participate in or benefit from the federally funded program or activity in question.[1] As discussed below, children who have AIDS, are HIV positive, are carriers of Hepatitis B or have other actual or perceived infectious conditions ordinarily meet both of these criteria for purposes of preschool, elementary and secondary education. Section 504 and its regulations then protect these children against such discriminatory practices as exclusion from school and overly restrictive or isolated placements ostensibly designed to protect others from transmission.

1. Children Who Have AIDS or are Carriers of Hepatitis B as "Otherwise Qualified" "Individuals with Handicaps"

"Individuals with Handicaps"　In the 1987 case of *School Board of Nassau County v. Arline*,[2] the Supreme Court ruled that individuals with actual or perceived infectious diseases may be protected "individuals with handicaps" under §504.[3] Since *Arline*, courts have consistently held (or, in some cases, assumed) that individuals who have tested positive for HIV or who have AIDS are covered by the anti-discrimination provisions of §504.[4] In some cases, courts found that the individuals before them were "individuals with handicaps" because

HIV infection in fact substantially limited them in a major life activity, as required by one prong of the §504 definition.[5] Others courts have based this determination upon that prong of the definition that encompasses individuals who "are regarded" as having an impairment that substantially limits a major life activity.[6]

Relying in part upon these cases, OCR has taken the position that virtually all children with AIDS or HIV positive status are "individual[s] with handicaps" within the meaning of §504.[7] OCR has also recognized status as a carrier of the Hepatitis B virus as a "handicap" triggering §504 coverage.[8]

"Otherwise Qualified" Section §504 does not contain a definition or explanation of the phrase "otherwise qualified." Department of Education regulations, however, provide that for purposes of public preschool, elementary or secondary school services and activities, a child "with handicaps" is "otherwise qualified" if she or he is of an age during which non-handicapped individuals are provided with such services, of an age during which it is mandatory under state law to provide such services to handicapped individuals, or is someone IDEA requires the state to provide with a free appropriate public education.[9] Virtually all school-age children who are HIV positive or who have symptoms of AIDS or who are carriers of Hepatitis B are thus "otherwise qualified" and so protected from discrimination by §504. They are entitled to all §504 protections, including the right to comparable benefits and services[10] and to attend the regular education or other classes they would have otherwise attended.

Judicial decisions to date involving discrimination against school age children with AIDS, HIV positive status and other infectious conditions, have, by and large, reached their decisions without reference to the regulatory definition of "otherwise qualified." Interpreting *Arline*, which involved employment discrimination rather than exclusion from public school, these courts have ruled that whether or not a child is an *"otherwise qualified* individual with handicaps" — and therefore protected by §504 at all — depends upon whether there is a realistic, significant risk to the health and safety of others under the particular circumstances, and whether reasonable steps might be taken to reduce that risk.[11] Under this analysis, the critical questions are how the risk of transmission is to be assessed, and how great that risk must be in order to justify exclusion or other unequal treatment.

2. Assessing Risk

In *Arline*, the Supreme Court identified four factors that must be considered in determining whether a particular individual poses a significant risk to the health and safety of others due to an infectious condition. The determination must be based upon reasonable medical judgments, given the current state of medical knowledge, about:

(1) the nature of the risk, i.e. the manner in which the disease is transmitted;

(2) the duration of the risk, i.e. how long the carrier is infectious;

(3) the severity of the risk, i.e. the potential harm to others; and

(4) the probability that the disease will be transmitted and will cause varying degrees of harm.[12]

The assessment of risk must be made on an individualized, case-by-case basis,[13] with deference given "to the reasonable medical judgments of public health officials."[14]

If, as a result of this analysis, it appears that a child's presence in school or participation in a particular classroom, program or activity poses a *significant* risk to the health and safety of others, the question then becomes whether reasonable accommodations can be made to reduce the risk to an "acceptable" level.[15] The probable effect of any accommodation on the child's psychological and educational development must be taken into account, along with his or her right to be educated, to the maximum extent appropriate, in the least restrictive environment.[16]

Section 504 does not permit schools or courts to require absolute certainty that others will face no risk whatsoever.[17] *Children with AIDS and other infectious conditions cannot be required to disprove every theoretical possibility of harm to others.*[18] Unless the risk of transmission and ensuing harm is *significant* under the particular circumstances *and* cannot be ameliorated by reasonable accommodations and precautions, children with AIDS, children who are carriers of Hepatitis B and others with infectious conditions cannot be excluded from school, isolated from other children while in school, or otherwise subjected to discrimination.[19]

Given such rigorous standards and current medical knowledge concerning AIDS, it is difficult to envision many, if any, circumstances under which exclusion will be permissible. These rules have already resulted in victories for children in a number of cases. In one Illinois case,[20] for example, the court ordered a school district to admit to the regular first grade classroom a 7 year old first grader who had been diagnosed as having AIDS Related Complex; the school system had so far refused to do so, placing him alone in an isolated, modular classroom. Another Illinois student excluded from school (as well as all extracurricular activities) and placed on homebound instruction when school officials discovered that he had AIDS obtained a preliminary injunction requiring his return to regular classes.[21] In California, a school district that expelled a kindergartner after he bit the clothing of another child was likewise ordered to allow him to return.[22] And in Florida, a child with mental retardation as well as AIDS successfully appealed a court order permitting her to attend school only if she were placed by herself in a glass room to be constructed within the special education classroom she was otherwise entitled to attend.[23] Children who are carriers of Hepatitis B have also successfully challenged efforts to isolate them or to exclude them from school.[24]

B. IDEA Issues

Children who are HIV positive or who have AIDS or other infectious conditions are not automatically "children with disabilities" within the meaning of IDEA, and so not automatically covered by that statute.[25] Where resulting health problems adversely affect educational performance (causing a need for "special education" as defined by IDEA), a child might be "other health impaired" as defined by IDEA and its regulations, and so one of the covered "children with disabilities."[26] Other children with infectious conditions might fall within IDEA on account of an additional disability that in and of itself triggers IDEA eligibility, such as mental retardation, severe emotional disturbance, blindness, traumatic brain injury, etc. IDEA rights and the §504 issues discussed above may become intertwined where, for example, school officials fearing AIDS transmission refuse to allow a child covered by IDEA to attend the educational program developed through the IEP process, or where the IEP itself calls for an overly restrictive placement (such as homebound study) simply because a child has AIDS.[27]

Any child meeting the IDEA definition of "children with disabilities" would, of course, have all of the substantive and procedural rights created by IDEA. Where the issue is exclusion from school, isolation or other unequal treatment on account of the fear of transmission, however, proceeding under IDEA may be more of a hindrance than help. As explained above in Chapter VI(F)(2), IDEA usually requires parents and children to exhaust administrative remedies before seeking relief from a court. Where children lose at the administrative level, or where school officials appeal a favorable administrative decision to court, illegal exclusion and discrimination can continue for far longer than they would if court proceedings were begun immediately. For example, in *Martinez v. School Board of Hillsborough County,*[28] the Florida case mentioned above, Eliana Martinez was refused admission to school in the summer of 1986; IDEA administrative proceedings resulted in a final order upholding the exclusion in August, 1987; after an unfavorable decision in federal district court and an appeal to the Eleventh Circuit Court of Appeals, she finally obtained a court order requiring school officials to allow her into the classroom in April, 1989.[29]

Even if a child is covered by IDEA, he or she should not be required to exhaust IDEA administrative remedies in order to challenge exclusion or other discrimination based upon fear of AIDS (or any other contagious condition) transmission. When a school system excludes a child with specific learning disabilities from school because she also happens to have AIDS, for example, it is not acting on the basis her educational needs. The dispute is not about the particular special education, related services and placement necessary to meet her unique needs as a student with learning disabilities, (and so required under IDEA), but rather about whether the school system may refuse to provide those services, thereby violating her IDEA rights, simply because she has AIDS. This is primarily a §504 issue. Students challenging attempts to exclude them from school should therefore be permitted to proceed directly to court on the §504 claims discussed above.[30]

Notes

1. 29 U.S.C. §794(a).

2. 480 U.S. 273 (1987).

3. 480 U.S. at 284-286. *Arline* involved a public school teacher with a history of tuberculosis who had been fired after a series of relapses. School board officials claimed that because they had fired her out of fear of contagion — and not because of any physical impairment associated with tuberculosis — she was not an "individual with handicaps" for purposes of §504. The court rejected this argument, holding that "the fact that a person

with a record of a physical impairment is also contagious does not suffice to remove that person from coverage under §504." *Id.*, 480 U.S. at 286. The court noted, however, that because tuberculosis in this case gave rise to both a physical impairment and to contagiousness, the case did not raise, and the court did not reach, "the questions of whether a carrier of a contagious disease such as AIDS could be considered to have a physical impairment, or whether such a person could be considered, solely on the basis of contagiousness, a handicapped person as defined by the Act." *Id.*, 480 U.S. at 282, n.7.

4. *See, e.g.*, Leckelt v. Board of Commissioners of Hospital District No. 1, 909 F.2d 820 (5th Cir. 1990); Martinez v. School Board of Hillsborough County, 861 F.2d 1502 (11th Cir. 1988); Chalk v. U.S. District Court Central District of California, 840 F.2d 701 (9th Cir. 1988); Doe v. Attorney General, 723 F. Supp. 452 (N.D. Cal. 1989); Doe v. Dolton Elementary School District No. 148, 694 F. Supp. 440 (N.D. Ill. 1988); Robertson v. Granite City Community Unit School District No. 9, 684 F. Supp. 1002 (S.D. Ill. 1988); Doe v. Belleville Public School District, 672 F. Supp. 342 (S.D. Ill. 1987); Ray v. School District of DeSoto County, 666 F. Supp. 1524 (M.D. Fla. 1987). For pre-*Arline* cases to the same effect, see Thomas v. Atascadero Unified School District, 662 F. Supp. 376 (C.D. Cal. 1987); District 27 Community School Board v. Board of Education of the City of New York, 130 Misc.2d. 398, 502 N.Y.S. 2d 325 (N.Y. Sup. Ct. 1986).

5. *See, e.g., Thomas*, 662 F. Supp at 379; *Martinez*, 861 F.2d at 1506; *Robertson*, 684 F. Supp. at 1007; *Doe v. Dolton*, 694 F. Supp. 444-45; *District 27 Community School Board*, 502 N.Y.S.2d at 336.

6. *See, e.g., Doe v. Dolton*, 694 F. Supp. at 443-44; *District 27 Community School Board*, 502 N.Y.S.2d at 336.

7. See OCR Staff Memorandum by William L. Smith, Acting Assistant Secretary for Civil Rights, April 5, 1990, reported at 16 EHLR 712. *See also* Sumter County (SC) School District #17, 17 EHLR 193 (OCR 9/28/90) (finding that school district discriminated against student with AIDS in imposing discipline, and so violated §504).

8. *See* Clare-Gladwin (MI) Intermediate School District, 16 EHLR 105 (OCR 7/13/89).

9. 34 C.F.R. §104.3(k).

10. See discussion in Chapters I(B)(2) and II(A)(2), *supra*.

11. *See Martinez*, 861 F.2d at 1505-06; *Doe v. Dolton*, 694 F. Supp. at 445; *Thomas*, 662 F. Supp. at 381-82.

12. 480 U.S. at 287-288.

13. *Id.*

14. *Id.* at 288.

15. *Id.*; *Martinez*, 861 F.2d at 1505-05.

16. *Martinez*, 861 F.2d. at 1506-1507. *Cf. New York State Association for Retarded Children*, 612 F.2d, 644, 650-51 (2nd Cir. 1979).

17. *Chalk*, 840 F.2d at 707.

18. *Id.* at 709. *See also Martinez*, 861 F.2d at 1506.

19. *See, e.g., Martinez*, 861 F.2d at 1506.

20. *Robertson, supra.*

21. *Doe v. Dolton, supra.*

22. *Thomas, supra.*

23. *Martinez, supra; see also opinion on remand*, 711 F. Supp. 1066 (M.D. Fla. 1989). Other cases vindicating the right of children with AIDS to attend school are among those cited in note 4, *supra*.

24. *See New York State Association for Retarded Children, supra* (segregating all previously institutionalized children who are Hepatitis B carriers would violate §504; mental retardation, rather than Hepatitis B status, identified as the "handicap" for purposes of §504 analysis); *but see* Kohl v. Woodhaven Learning Center, 865 F.2d 930 (8th Cir. 1989), *cert. denied*, 110 S. Ct. 239 (1989) (adult services program did not violate §504 by refusing to serve developmentally disabled adult who was hepatitis B carrier and exhibited certain "maladaptive behaviors"; reasonable accommodations would not sufficiently reduce risk of transmission).

25. *Belleville Public School District*, 672 F. Supp. at 344-45; *District 27 Community School Board*, 502 N.Y.S. 2d at 339; Inquiry of Barnes, EHLR 211:343 (OSEP 9/27/84).

26. *Belleville Public School District*, 672 F. Supp. at 344-45; *Inquiry of Barnes* at EHLR 211:344. For a general discussion of the disability categories and criteria triggering IDEA coverage, see Chapter I(A)(1), *supra*.

27. In a pre-*Arline* case, an Illinois court resolved similar issues as strictly a least restrictive environment/mainstreaming matter under IDEA (then known as the EAHCA), with no mention of §504. In Community High School District 155 v. Denz, 79 Ill. Dec. 444, 463 N.E.2d 998 (Ill. App. Ct. 1984), the school system attempted to place a student with Downs Syndrome who was also an asymptomatic carrier of Hepatitis B on homebound instruction, rather than placing her in the special education program she would have attended but for the Hepatitis B. School officials claimed that in view of her medical condition, homebound instruction was the least restrictive environment for her pursuant to IDEA. The student had prevailed at a due process hearing, at the due process review, and before the state trial court on the claim that homebound placement violated her IDEA right to placement in the least restrictive environment. After discussing IDEA's least restrictive environment requirements and assessing the risk that the student would transmit Hepatitis B to others, the appellate court upheld these earlier decisions. See 463 N.E.2d at 1003-04.

28. 861 F.2d 1502 (11th Cir. 1988); on remand 711 F. Supp. 1066 (M.D. Fla. 1989).

29. Eliana Martinez had mental retardation as well as AIDS, and was refused enrollment in a special education classroom when she first applied for admission to public school. It is unclear whether she attempted to assert her "stay put" rights under 20 U.S.C. §1415(e)(3) in order to secure admission pending the lengthy proceedings that ensued. Section 1415(e)(3) provides:

> "During the pendency of any proceedings conducted pursuant to this section, unless the State or local educational agency and the parents or guardian otherwise agree, the child shall remain in the then current educational placement of such child, or, *if applying for initial admission to a public school, shall, with the consent of the parents or guardian, be placed in the public school program until all such proceedings have been completed.*"

(Emphasis added).

30. *Cf. Robertson*, 648 F. Supp. at 1005 (IDEA [then EAHCA] not applicable to child whose learning and behavioral problems were not result of his hemophilia or ARC; IDEA exhaustion not required, plaintiff permitted to proceed on §504 claims); *also Martinez*, 861 F.2d at 1506 (where parties agreed on placement that would be appropriate for child with mental retardation under IDEA [then EHA] but for her AIDS, question was whether exclusion from that setting violates §504). As noted in the text above, the child in *Martinez* did raise IDEA claims and did exhaust administrative remedies before bringing an action in court. The court thus was not called upon to decide whether exhaustion of IDEA administrative remedies was required and/or whether Eliana could have proceeded simply under §504.

Assuming, for sake of argument, that IDEA exhaustion requirements were applied, children with AIDS should still be excused from exhausting administrative remedies on the ground that time-consuming exhaustion is an inadequate remedy (a traditional exception to the exhaustion doctrine - see Chapter VI, above) for a child with a life-threatening condition. Administrative remedies may be inadequate and exhaustion therefore excused when it "will work severe harm upon a litigant." Christopher W. v. Portsmouth School Committee, 877 F.2d 1089, 1094-95 (1st Cir. 1989) (citations omitted). In addition, the rationale underlying the IDEA exhaustion requirement, *i.e.* "considerations of agency expertise" and "accuracy," *Christopher W.*, 877 F.2d at 1095, have little if any relevance in the context of AIDS-based discrimination, which involves public health and medical issues rather than educational ones. State education agencies and due process hearing officers have no more expertise in these matters than do the courts.

As explained in Chapter VI(F)(2), above, IDEA exhaustion requirements may apply to §504 claims under certain circumstances. The exhaustion issues discussed herein may therefore arise (or be raised by school systems) even where children who have been excluded, isolated or otherwise discriminated against do not raise IDEA claims.

VIII.
Discipline of Students With Disabilities

The various laws protecting students with disabilities place limitations on school officials administering discipline, particularly the circumstances in which students can be excluded unilaterally from their current educational placements through long term disciplinary suspension or expulsion. The substantive rights discussed above, namely, the right to an appropriate public education[1] in the least restrictive environment,[2] the right to have all changes in placement take place through prescribed procedures,[3] and the right to remain in one's current educational placement during complaint proceedings,[4] all limit the extent to which school officials may impose disciplinary exclusions on students who have been identified as disabled, those with evaluations or appeals pending, and students who may be perceived as having a disability.[5]

Prior to the enactment of IDEA and §504, courts recognized the rights of children with disabilities to receive a publicly supported education and established the principle that exclusion on the basis of disability is unconstitutional on federal due process and equal protection grounds,[6] and on state constitutional and statutory grounds.[7]

A. The Federal Statutory Entitlements

As evidenced by their legislative histories, the substantive and procedural rights provided to eligible pupils under IDEA and §504 were intended to protect them from being constructively excluded from public school as well as being subject to long-term and indefinite suspensions and expulsions.

While courts generally consider disciplinary matters to be within the discretionary authority of state and local school authorities, courts have construed these two federal statutes and their implementing regulations as placing substantive and procedural limits on state power to discipline students with disabilities.

Significantly, disabled students, as other students facing possible suspension, are entitled to procedural due process.[8] Where an emergency situation justifies a delay in the normal hearing procedures prior to a suspension, a preliminary hearing must be held as soon as practicable, and in no case later than seventy-two hours after the removal of the student from her current educational placement.[9]

Continuation of the suspension of a disabled student whose conduct is related to her disabling condition[s] should be permitted only so long as the emergency situation exists. A finding to the contrary violates the individual's right not to be discriminated against on the basis of disability under §504, and not to be punished on the basis of one's status and in the absence of personal culpability.[10] As will be discussed below, no student with an IEP or with a pending evaluation, complaint or appeal can be suspended by school authorities for more than ten days without violating the entitlements under IDEA, regardless of whether a nexus exists between their disability and their misconduct.

1. The right to an appropriate public education

Many federal courts have enjoined school districts from expelling or constructively excluding students with disabilities for "misbehavior" based, in part, on finding that the exclusion violated the student's right to a free appropriate education.[11]

In one federal action where the record before the court clearly suggested that the school had failed to provide a disabled student with an appropriate individualized education, the court acknowledged that the school's "handling of the plaintiff may have contributed to her disruptive behavior."[12] If, the court stated, a subsequent placement team found that "plaintiff had not been given an appropriate special education placement, defendant's resort to its disciplinary process is unjustifiable." [13]

2. The right to have any "change in placement" occur through prescribed procedures

A second legal ground for challenging a disciplinary exclusion of a student protected under IDEA and/or §504 rests on the right to have any "change in placement" occur only through the prescribed procedures. Under applicable statutory and regulatory provisions, parents must be notified in writing within a reasonable time before a school district proposes to "change the placement" of a student with disabilities under IDEA and/or §504.[14]

Prior to the 1988 decision by the United States Supreme Court in *Honig v. Doe*,[15] a long line of cases held that expulsions and indefinite exclusions of students with disabilities constitute unlawful changes in placement.[16] A number of courts had held or stated that a short-term (emergency) suspension for up to ten school days did not constitute a "change in placement" necessitating the procedural safeguards of IDEA and/or §504.[17] Other courts had interpreted a change in placement as a modification that affects the learning experience of the disabled child in some significant way.[18] The Supreme Court in *Honig*, addressing for the first time the parameters for excluding disabled students under IDEA, clarified the meaning of a "change in placement" when it ruled that school officials could not unilaterally subject students with disabilities to long-term disciplinary exclusions. Rather, the Court required school officials to treat an exclusion of more than ten school days as a "change in placement" within IDEA, and to provide students the procedural safeguards mandated when proposing a "change in placement" under IDEA. In adopting this standard, the Court deferred to the interpretation of the Office of Special Educational Programs of the U.S. Department of Education.[19] Parenthetically, the Court noted that the Department's position was first espoused by its Office for Civil Rights in 1980, when OCR interpreted suspensions of more than ten school days cumulatively in a school year to be a significant change in placement under §504.[20]

Under IDEA the notice required prior to any "change in placement" must explain all procedural rights available to the parents and describe the proposed action, the basis for the school's decision, other options considered, and the reasons for their rejection.[21] This notice must be comprehensible to the parents, be in the parents' native language unless clearly not feasible, and be otherwise effectively communicated where the parent's mode of communication is not a written language.[22] The regulations implementing §504 require recipient school districts to implement a system of procedural safeguards that includes notice, an opportunity to be heard by an impartial decision maker, representation by counsel, a review procedure, and explicitly note that "[c]ompliance with the procedural safeguards of section 615 of [IDEA] is one means of meeting this requirement."[23]

Responsibility for changing a disabled child's education placement, including removal from her current educational placement through suspension, rests with the members of the child's IEP team[24] with parental participation, after consideration of the child's needs, evaluation data, current program and placement, and placement options.[25] The school district must make a concerted effort to ensure parental participation, including proper notification of the meeting, agreement in scheduling, alternative means of participation, and actions to insure that the parent understands the proceedings. If warranted, or if the child's parent or teacher requests it, the child for whom a change of placement is being considered shall also be reevaluated.[26] Consistent with the regulations implementing §504, a recipient school district must reevaluate a student who is an "individual with handicaps" under §504, who may or may not also be protected by IDEA, prior to making any "significant change in [her] placement."[27]

IDEA does not require parental consent prior to changing the placement of a disabled student who is receiving special education. However, after receiving notice of the proposed change of placement, the parent has a right to complain about the proposed educational placement and/or provision of free appropriate public education to the child.[28] Furthermore, the parent has the right to an impartial hearing concerning any complaint, including any proposal to change the child's placement or any matter concerning the provision of free appropriate public education to such child.[29]

In summary, exclusion beyond ten days, regardless of the reason, is sufficiently lengthy to constitute a change in the student's current educational placement, which can only be accomplished through the proper change-in-placement procedures, including, as will be discussed below, a determination by a properly constituted team that the current placement is no longer the least restrictive, development of a new plan for appropriate education in the least restrictive environment, and protection of educational status pending the proceedings.

3. The right to be educated in the least restrictive environment

Both IDEA and §504 guarantee students with disabilities the right to participate in regular classroom and extracurricular activities with non-disabled students to the greatest extent practicable while receiving an appropriate education.[30] The IDEA, which describes this right in terms of the "least restrictive environment," requires assurances by state and local education agencies that "special classes, separate schooling, or other removal of handicapped children from the regular education environment occurs only when the nature or severity of the handicap is such that education in regular classes with the use of supplementary aids and services cannot be achieved satisfactorily."[31] The language of §504 regulation 34 C.F.R. §104.34(a) is very similar.

Because students with disabilities have an independent right to be "mainstreamed" or integrated with nondisabled peers to the greatest extent appropriate under IDEA and §504, courts have enjoined school officials from removing them from their educational placements.[32] For example, one court determined that a student, if expelled, would suffer irreparable harm because she would be precluded from participating in any special education programs offered at the school. Her placement options would, the court indicated, be restricted to private school or to homebound tutoring. The court expressed concern that if the former were unavailable, her education would be reduced to homebound tutoring, which "can only serve to hinder plaintiff's social development and perpetuate the vicious cycle in which she is caught."[33] Reasoning that a long-term suspension or expulsion from school may prevent a disabled student from being placed in a program that is appropriate for her academic and social development, this same court found that "[t]his result flies in the face of the explicit mandate of the [IDEA] which requires that all placement decisions be made in conformity with a child's right to an education in the least restrictive environment."[34]

In holding that the right to a free appropriate education in the least restrictive environment foreclosed expulsions and limited suspensions to those of brief duration, pre-*Honig* lower court decisions specifically recognized the "change in placement" procedures under IDEA as replacing expulsion as a means of removing children with disabilities from school who are dangerous or seriously disruptive.[35] This analysis is supported by *Honig's* holding that a long-term disciplinary exclusion is a "change of placement" within the meaning of IDEA, and by the Court's recognition that a disabled child's IEP is the "primary vehicle" for implementing IDEA's mandate — including the obligation to provide special education in the least restrictive environment.[36] The least restrictive environment mandate is implemented, in part, by requiring schools to provide a continuum of alternative education placements, in which each child receives an education appropriate to her individual needs while maximizing interaction with her non-disabled peers.[37] Indeed, the comment to the regulation implementing the least restrictive environment requirement of IDEA (and §504) explicitly contemplates the use of such an approach, reading as follows:

> ". . .it should be stressed that, where a handicapped child is so disruptive in a regular classroom that the education of other students is significantly impaired, the needs of the handicapped child cannot be met in that environment.

Therefore regular placement would not be appropriate to his or her needs . . ."[38]

4. The right to remain in one's current educational placement under the "stay-put" provision

What is often referred to as IDEA's "stay put" provision states that:

> "During the pendency of any proceedings conducted pursuant to this section, unless the state or local education agency and the parents or guardians otherwise agree, the child *shall remain* in the then current educational placement of such child, or, if applying for initial admission to a public school shall, with the consent of the parents or guardian, be placed in the public school program until all such proceedings have been completed."[39]

Who is covered? Section 1415 of Title 20, referenced by the above quoted subsection (e)(3), includes provisions concerning any proposal to initiate or change or refusal to initiate or change the identification, evaluation, or placement of the child or the provision of a free appropriate public education.[40] It also provides that a parent is entitled to complain "with respect to any matter relating to the identification, evaluation, or educational placement of the child, or the provision of a free appropriate public education to such child..."[41]; that the parent has a right to a hearing concerning any complaint or, alternatively, concerning any proposal to initiate or change or refusal to initiate or change the identification, evaluation, or educational placement of the child or the provision of a free appropriate education.[42] Other provisions concern procedural safeguards, appeals and judicial actions.

Based on the statutory language quoted above, the right to remain in one's current educational placement encompasses students once they are referred for an evaluation though they have not yet been identified as disabled and in need of special education under the Act. The regulation implementing this statutory provision is, it should be argued, under inclusive compared to the broad statutory language of §1415(e)(3). The regulatory provision limits the status quo to be maintained only "[d]uring the pendency of any administrative or judicial proceeding regarding a complaint unless the parents of the child agree otherwise. . ."[43]

Rules of statutory construction and public policy favor the broad statutory construction, treating the evaluation process as a "proceeding" within the meaning of §1415(e)(3), IDEA's "stay-put" provision. Given the overall purpose and intent of the law[44] and the affirmative duty of the state and local school districts to identify and evaluate students suspected of being disabled under IDEA[45] and §504[46], it makes little sense to change the placement of a student who has been referred for an evaluation for special education services during the evaluation process.[47]

Filing an administrative due process complaint under 20 U.S.C. §1415(b), whether challenging the suspension of a student who has been referred for an evaluation (but not yet determined to have a disability and be in need of special education) under IDEA, or the identification, evaluation or program of a previously classified disabled student, should entitle the parent to an impartial hearing.[48] During the pendency of all proceedings concerning that complaint, the student is entitled to continue in her current educational placement.[49]

How has the U.S. Supreme Court interpreted the "stay-put" provision? In *Honig v. Doe*, the U.S. Supreme Court addressed for the first time the apparent conflict between the so-called "stay-put" provision and disciplinary procedures of public schools.[50] The Court accepted review of an appellate decision affirming that absent parental consent, there were no exceptions to a student's right to remain in her current educational placement under §1415(e)(3) of IDEA. The case stemmed from an action challenging the indefinite suspensions of two emotionally disturbed students[51] who were excluded from a special school for disabled youth because they were considered dangerous and disruptive. Rejecting the dangerousness exception argued by the State of California, Justice Brennan, writing for a 6 - 2 majority, stated that the express language of §1415(e)(3) is "unequivocal" and contains no emergency exception for a dangerous or disruptive student.[52] Citing also the legislative history of the Act to support Congress' intent to educate all disabled students, including those with severe behavioral problems,[53] the Court forcefully pronounced, "We think it clear. . .that Congress very much meant to strip schools of the unilateral authority they had traditionally employed to exclude disabled students, particularly emotionally disturbed students from school."[54]

The Court, however, recognized that Congress did not leave school administrators powerless to deal with dangerous students, referring to a comment to the regulations, which, in essence, states that while a child's placement may not be changed during the pendency of any complaint proceedings, a school district is not precluded from using its normal procedures for dealing with children who are endangering themselves or others.[55] Several such procedures were identified by the majority to address this "emergency" situation, including the use of study carrels, timeouts, detention, or restriction of privileges. In addition, the Court allowed that when a student poses an immediate threat of injury to self or others, school officials may temporarily suspend her for up to ten (10) school days without changing the student's educational placement. This time frame permits school administrators to protect the safety of others while using this opportunity to initiate an IEP review (for purposes of reviewing the appropriateness of the student's program and placement) and seek, if necessary, parental consent to an interim placement.[56]

Ruling, however, that the "stay-put" provision does not "operate to limit the equitable powers of district courts such that they cannot, in appropriate cases, temporarily enjoin a dangerous child from attending school",[57] the Court opened the door for school officials to seek injunctive relief in certain limited instances. Although *Honig* characterized the burden on school districts seeking to overcome the strong presumption of continued placement created by §1415(e)(3) as "substantial" - one overcome only by showing that maintaining the child's placement is "substantially likely to result in injury either to himself, herself, or to others,"[58] recent case law suggests that at least in the context of so-called discipline situations,[59] courts are applying a standard that is more favorable to school officials. Courts are not giving presumptive weight to §1415(e)(3); they are neither requiring a showing of the emergency standard of injury to self/others, nor sufficiently considering the cumulative weight to be accorded the other statutory entitlements of IDEA and §504, as directed by the Supreme Court,[60] when balanced against the school district's case for exclusion.[61]

What is meant by "current educational placement"? The term "current educational placement" as used in §1415(e)(3) has been interpreted to include the last placement of a disabled child agreed to by the child's parents (and appropriately provided for by the school district);[62] the child's last lawful placement;[63] the general type of educational placement in which the child is placed, rather than referring to a specific program or school;[64] and the "education and related services provided in accordance with the child's most recent individualized education program."[65]

No court, however, has recognized a disabled youth's "expulsion" or "suspension" status, i.e., no educational program, as a "current educational placement" within the meaning of IDEA. Such an interpretation would be circular and in violation of the legislative intent and express statutory language of §1415(e)(3) as construed by the *Honig* court.[66] In fact, the Court of Appeals for the Fifth Circuit has held that school officials who withhold educational services to disabled students excluded from school for disciplinary reasons violate those students' right to a free appropriate public education,[67] and the United States Department of Education has adopted this reasoning.[68]

Finally, to summarize the claim under §1415(e)(3), during the pendency of any proceedings (including change-of-placement proceedings), the student should remain in her current educational placement, except under the emergency conditions described above.

5. The right not to be punished on the basis of disability or for the school district's failure to provide an appropriate education

School authorities may not suspend or impose other disciplinary sanctions on students with disabilities or students referred for evaluation when the conduct for which the measures are being considered is an element of, or related to, the student's disability or is the result of an inappropriate educational program or placement. Any such action is challengeable under the statutory entitlements of IDEA, the nondiscrimination provisions of §504, and the equal protection and due process clauses of the Fourteenth Amendment.[69]

As explained above, any disciplinary sanction that violates a disabled student's right to IDEA's statutory entitlements is a per se violation of the Act. In such case, proof of a "nexus" between the student's misbehavior and his or her handicapping condition should be unnecessary.[70] When there is evidence of an actual or perceived link between a student's disability and misbehavior resulting in disciplinary sanctions, the student should also assert that such sanction violates her right under §504 to be free from discrimination on the basis of disability.[71]

Where there is evidence of nexus between a student's disability and conduct: Students whose objectionable behaviors are causally related to their disabilities should not under Section 504 be punished or suspended except in an emergency.[72] Section 504 prohibits by its very terms any recipient of federal financial assistance from discriminating against a disabled person (or a person regarded as disabled or with a record of having a disability) on the basis of her disability.[73] Regulations implementing §504 make it clear that no disabled person should be denied appropriate education "regardless of the nature and severity of the person's handicap,"[74] that an "appropriate education" must be designed to meet individual educational needs of handicapped persons as adequately as the needs of nonhandicapped persons are met. . .";[75] and that such education must be provided with non-disabled students to the "maximum extent appropriate."[76] These provisions reflect the legislative intent not to treat disabled persons disparately; other implementing regulations explicitly proscribe discriminating against persons within the protection of §504's definition on the basis of disability.[77]

OCR policy prohibits suspensions of ten days or more or a series of suspensions totalling ten days or more during a school year, or the expulsion of students with disabilities when the behavior for which suspension and/or expulsion is being considered is an element of or related to the student's disabling condition or the result of inappropriate educational program or placement.[78] A strong argument can, nonetheless, be made based on the non-discrimination language of §504 itself and its explicit regulations barring discrimination on the basis of disability, that any non-emergency suspension or exclusion under ten days consecutively or cumulatively is unlawful.

Where an inappropriate educational program and/or placement is related to punishable behaviors: School officials who fail to provide disabled students with an appropriate education and then discipline those students for behaviors that are causally linked to the inappropriate educational programming and placement decisions violate both IDEA and the above described provisions of §504 and its implementing regulations. A number of courts have relied upon these laws in holding that school authorities may not lawfully impose disciplinary sanctions on students for conduct which may be a result of the school's own failure to have provided an appropriate educational program or placement.[79] Courts have similarly held that punishing a student for conduct which is related to her disability or the school's failure to provide an appropriate program designed to meet her unique needs violates the student's right not to be punished in the absence of personal guilt.[80]

6. The rights of students never classified or referred for evaluation

Students who have disabilities and are in need of special education
Many students who engage in persistent misbehavior are in fact
disabled under the definitions of IDEA, §504, or state statutes which
may be broader in scope. Schools may label such students as
"behavioral problems" for purposes of excluding them from the regular
education program through suspension, expulsion, or transfer to so-
called alternative education programs (e.g., for the "socially
maladjusted").[81] School officials who label such students as
"behavioral problems" instead of referring them for evaluations may be
deliberately seeking to obviate their affirmative obligations under the
federal disability statutes to identify, locate and evaluate all children
with disabilities residing within their jurisdictions,[82] and to provide
those needing special education and related services with full,
individualized evaluations of their needs.[83] It should be argued that
it is illegal to suspend or expel any such student for misbehavior - with
the sole exception of an emergency short-term emergency suspension -
if the student who has never been identified as disabled or referred for
an evaluation has or is reasonably suspected of having a disabling
condition.[84] This is consistent with the argument *supra*, contending
that only in the case of an emergency may school authorities suspend
a disabled individual whose disability has a causal relationship to the
behavior for which he is being punished.

In *Rodriguez v. Board of Education of the Cato-Meridien Central
School District*,[85] plaintiff, a student not classified as disabled who
required medication to control epileptic-type seizures, obtained a
temporary restraining order based on §504, enjoining his exclusion
from school following a confrontation with the principal. The youth
had difficulty controlling his temper in stressful situations; stress
increased the frequency of seizures. Though defendants were aware of
his condition, the complaint alleged they had never referred him for an
evaluation under IDEA and/or §504, nor attempted to provide
assistance in addressing his emotional needs. Plaintiff's school record
during the 1½ years preceding his complaint reflected several
instances when he was suspended from school for lack of control.

***Students with serious behavioral difficulties who are treated as if
they are disabled*** Students with serious behavioral difficulties, who
may or may not be in need of special education, but who are denied the
opportunity to participate in regular education programs because they

are treated as, or perceived as having disabilities are protected by §504.[86]

A student whose behavior is sufficiently serious to warrant exclusion from school for a lengthy period of time may arguably be being treated by school officials as if she were "handicapped." Substantive due process requires that the punishment imposed for behavior problems in school be reasonably related to a public school's obligation under the education clause of its state constitution and state statutes (including compulsory education laws) to educate all children. The school's interest in excluding a student for a lengthy period of time must outweigh the student's right to be educated under state law.[87] Any serious disparity between the offense and the punishment imposed may be challengeable as a violation of substantive due process.[88] The student may fall within §504 because school officials are treating her as if she were, for example, seriously emotionally disturbed,[89] or alternatively, may, if her behavioral difficulties are, in fact, so severe as to warrant such a harsh penalty, come within one of the definitions for eligibility under §504 or IDEA (e.g. seriously emotionally disturbed; mental/emotional illness which limits her ability to learn).

This argument may be buttressed by examining the student's record for notations reflecting the manner in which she is perceived by school authorities (e.g., "incorrigible," "amoral," "emotionally maladjusted," "disruptive,").[90] By identifying and labelling students as "behavior problems," schools may be removing/excluding students from the regular school program without complying with the substantive provisions of IDEA.

Another example in which students are treated as disabled but are constructively excluded from receiving an appropriate education concerns the use of alternative educational programs. Some states have established alternative education programs for students with behavior problems who are stigmatized and labelled "socially maladjusted" because this category is expressly excluded from the categorical definition "seriously emotionally disturbed."[91] Although these programs function as separate special education programs, where school districts ignore all evaluation, programming, and placement requirements of the federal statutes, an argument can be made that these students are being treated as disabled by school authorities and thus, are entitled to the protections of §504. Once established that these students come within the broad definition of §504, they are protected by its broad prohibitions against discrimination and are due its affirmative mandates.[92]

Students who use drugs and alcohol Regulations implementing
§504 previously encompassed individuals suffering from drug addiction
and substance abuse within its protected class of persons to the degree
their condition resulted in a substantial limitation of one or more
major life activities. The comments to the regulations implementing
§504 clarified that no student may be excluded from education solely
by reason of the presence or history of these conditions, and to the
extent the condition interfered with the person's meeting the basic
requirements of the program, the condition must be addressed.[93] An
elementary or secondary age student could not be excluded from school
on the basis of addiction or alcoholism, but rather was required to be
provided such education and related services, including counseling and
non-medical treatment as was needed to meet his needs.[94]

In 1990, the Americans with Disabilities Act (ADA) amended
Section 7(8) of the Rehabilitation Act of 1973[95] to exclude from the
definition of "individual with handicaps" those persons "...currently
engaging in the illegal use of drugs, when a covered entity acts on the
basis of such use." This exclusion does not exclude from the protections
of §504 1) those who have successfully completed a supervised drug
rehabilitation program, or have otherwise been rehabilitated, and are
no longer engaging in illegal drug use; 2) those who are participating
in a supervised drug rehabilitation program and are no longer
engaging in illegal drug use; or 3) those who erroneously are regarded
as engaging in illegal drug use, but are not engaging in such use.[96]
Congress further amended the Rehabilitation Act to speak specifically
to application of school discipline to instances of drug and alcohol
abuse. Significantly, students using alcohol are not excluded from the
definition of "individual[s] with handicaps" under §504. The
amendment authorizes local educational agencies to take disciplinary
action regarding the "use or possession of illegal drugs or alcohol
against any handicapped student who currently is engaging in the
illegal use of drugs and alcohol to the same extent that such
disciplinary action is taken against nonhandicapped students.
Furthermore, the due process procedures at 34 C.F.R.§104.36 shall not
apply to such disciplinary actions."[97]

If a student protected only under §504, who does not qualify as a
child with disabilities in need of special education under IDEA, is
found by school authorities to be "currently engaging in the illegal use
of drugs or alcohol," (note, possession alone is not enough), then the
student can be subject to normal school discipline procedures in
accordance with school guidelines and rules. Under this provision,
both drug and alcohol using students lose their rights to a reevaluation

before any significant change in placement[98] and impartial due process hearing and review consistent with the regulatory provisions of §504.[99] This amendment does not interfere with either student's constitutional right to due process.[100] Moreover, the alcohol using student would continue to be eligible to receive appropriate education and related services, including alcohol-related counseling, during the period of any exclusion.

On the other hand, if this student with disabilities comes within the eligibility criteria of both §504 and IDEA, then while he may waive his rights to his procedural protections under §504, he would not on the basis of this amendment to the Rehabilitation Act lose the protections afforded him by IDEA. In other words, he could not be unilaterally removed from school via suspension or other exclusion for a period in excess of ten school days without a court order finding him to be dangerous to himself or others. Furthermore, as discussed below, during the period of any exclusion the school would arguably be required to provide him with his right to an appropriate education. Also once this student evidences that at present he has ceased to engage in the illegal use of drugs and alcohol, he is no longer a current user, and once again becomes eligible for the protections of §504, including affirmative obligations on the part of the school district to assist him in addressing an impairment that interferes with a major life activity. Arguably, a school district that refused to admit to school a "former" drug or alcohol user or abuser would be discriminating on the basis of disability in violation of §504.

B. Unresolved Issues

1. The existence of a nexus between disabling conditions and [mis]conduct under IDEA

When a student, who is classified as disabled or who has been referred for evaluation under IDEA, challenges her suspension or disciplinary sanction on the basis of her statutory entitlements (as described above), it should not be necessary for her to demonstrate or prove a nexus between the conduct for which she is being punished and her disability.[101]

The Supreme Court did not have occasion to address the issue of nexus in *Honig* because it was uncontested that the individual claimants were emotionally disturbed youth who had been unilaterally subjected to indefinite suspensions on the basis of dangerous and disruptive behavior that was related to their disabilities. It may, nonetheless, be possible to take some guidance from the Court's statutory interpretation of IDEA. Therein, the Court strictly construed the express statutory language of the "stay-put" provision by refusing to permit a "dangerousness" exception to be read into the statute. It emphasized that the language of §1415(e)(3) is "unequivocal" and "means what it says."[102] It also drew upon the legislative history of the Act specifically to support the principle that all disabled students, including those with the most severe behavioral problems, are the intended beneficiaries of the Act.[103] Any attempt to condition continuation of a student's broad entitlements under IDEA on proof of a causal nexus between disabling condition(s) and conduct merely facilitates exclusions which, as the Court recognized in *Honig*, Congress specifically intended to eliminate and prevent.[104] Nothing in the language of the Act explicitly or implicitly suggests conditioning, for example, the right to an appropriate education upon such a standard that would force school districts into a difficult, costly, and problematical causal inquiry into the relationship between disability and behavior.[105]

Court decisions interpreting IDEA to require state and local school districts to provide students with disabilities appropriate educational services for the duration of their up-to-ten days exclusions, or during any more extensive period allowed under a court ordered change in placement,[106] also undercut arguments that proof of nexus is required. Students with disabilities are guaranteed by federal and state statutes a full and appropriate public education which cannot be forfeited by a change in placement occasioned by behavior or conduct unrelated to disabling conditions. Regardless of their status, students who are disabled under IDEA and/or §504, even students who are incarcerated[107] or otherwise in the custody of other state agencies,[108] are entitled to receive their substantive special education related rights.

2. The abuse and inappropriate use of juvenile courts by school districts

An invidious tactic increasingly employed by some school districts is to file petitions for truancy, "children in need of services" (CHINS), and delinquency in the juvenile or family courts as a means of removing students who often have serious social, emotional and behavioral problems.[109] These types of cases frequently involve different state agencies and competing provisions of state law, and turn on rulings based on jurisdictional determinations.[110]

A recent decision by a state appellate court found that a local school district which filed an "unruly" petition in juvenile court against a mentally retarded, emotionally disturbed child in response to the youth's refusal to do classroom work and having threatened his teachers, violated IDEA and state special education laws and regulations.[111] The court found that the school district failed to meet the procedural requirements for changing the youth's educational placement, which occurred as a result of the unruly petition being filed and the youth placed into the juvenile court system. Relying on *Honig*, the court found that "[s]chool discipline problems and a student's failure to perform work must be addressed within the administrative framework of the school system before the school system can resort to court intervention."[112]

3. The duty to educate during the period of exclusion

In 1981, the Court of Appeals for the Fifth Circuit in *S-1 v. Turlington*[113] ruled that to the degree expulsion was "a proper disciplinary tool,. . . [under IDEA and §504]. . .a complete cessation of educational services" was not.[114] Although the Court of Appeals for the Sixth Circuit followed this ruling,[115] the Ninth Circuit may have parted company when it suggested in *Doe v. Maher*,[116] albeit in *dicta*, that "[i]f the child's misbehavior is properly determined not to be a manifestation of his handicap,"[117] the disabled child can be expelled, and consequently denied educational services.[118] *Doe v. Maher* was appealed to the Supreme Court, resulting in the *Honig* decision discussed above. However, because the appellees were emotionally disturbed youth who had been indefinitely excluded from a special segregated school on the basis of their behavioral disorders, the Supreme Court had no reason to reach this issue in *Honig*. However, given the Court's finding that the plain language of §1415(e)(3) "means what it says" and the right of a student with disabilities to remain in her current educational placement is "unequivocal", it is not a far stretch to argue that the Court should similarly interpret §1412(1) to obligate each participating state to provide each student with disabilities within its jurisdiction a free appropriate public education during the period of any lawful exclusion,[119] and to interpret the other entitlements of IDEA, as discussed above, to preclude the use of expulsion as "a proper disciplinary tool."

Notes

1. 20 U.S.C.§§1401(16),(18), 1412(1),(2); 34 C.F.R.§§300.1, 300.4, 300.13 - 300.14, 300.121; 34 C.F.R. §104.33(b).

2. 20 U.S.C.§§1412(5)(B), 1414(a)(1)(C)(iv); 34 C.F.R. §300.132, 300.227, 300.550 - 553; 34 C.F.R.§104.34(a)

3. 20 U.S.C. §1415(b)(1)(C),(D); 34 C.F.R.§300.504(1),(b)(1)(ii); 34 C.F.R. §104.36.

4. 20 U.S.C.§1415(e)(3); 34 C.F.R. §300.513.

5. 20 U.S.C.§1400, 29 U.S.C.§794, 34 C.F.R. §104.4(a), (b).

6. Pennsylvania Association for Retarded Citizens v. Pennsylvania, 334 F. Supp. 279 (1972); Mills v. Board of Education of District of Columbia, 348 F. Supp. 866 (D.D.C. 1972).

7. *See, e.g.*, In re G.H., 218 N.W.2d 441 (North Dakota Supreme Ct. 1974); Frederick L. v. Thomas, 408 F. Supp. 832, 419 F. Supp. 960 (E.D. Pa. 1976), *aff'd* 557 F.2d 373 (3rd Cir. 1977).

8. Goss v. Lopez, 419 U.S. 565 (1975) (recognizing that the impact of an exclusion of ten days or less from school was "not *de minimis*" given students' "property interest" in education (created by state statutes) and "liberty interests" in their "good name, reputation, honor or integrity..." and requiring notice and an informal due process hearing before a disciplinary suspension or other exclusion, except in an emergency. *Id.*, at 582.

9. *Id.*, 419 U.S. at 582-83, 95 S. Ct. at 740 (hearing should be held "as soon as practicable, as the District Court indicated" - district court had set 72 hours after removal as outside limit for hearing; see 372 F. Supp. 1279, 1302); Doe v. Rockingham Co. School Bd., 658 F. Supp. 403, 407-80 (W.D. Va. 1987).

10. Courts have held it to be a violation of equal protection under the Fourteenth Amendment, U.S. Constitution, to penalize persons for their status or characteristics over which they have no control. *See e.g.*, Weber v. Aetna Casualty & Surety Co., 406 U.S. 164, 175 (1972) (illegitimacy); Harper v.Virginia Board of Education, 383 U.S. 663 (1966) (indigence); Plyler v. Doe, U.S. (1982) (parents' conduct; parents' alienage).

11. *See, e.g.*, Honig v. Doe, 108 S.Ct. 592 (1988), *affirming as mod.* Doe v. Maher, 793 F.2d 1470 (9th Cir. 1986); S-1 v. Turlington, No.78-8020-Civ-CA-WPB (S.D. Fla. June 15, 1979), *affirmed*, 635 F.2d 342 (5th Cir. 1981), *cert. denied* 454 U.S. 1030 (1981); Kaelin v. Grubbs, 682 F.2d 595 (6th Cir. 1982); School Board of Prince William County v. Malone, 762 F.2d 1120 (4th Cir. 1985); Stuart v. Nappi, 443 F. Supp. 1235 (D.Ct. 1978); Howard S. v. Friendswood Independent School District, 454 F. Supp. 634 (S.D. Tex. 1978); Doe v. Koger, 480 F. Supp. 225 (N.D. Ind. 1979); Sherry v. New York State Education Department, 479 F. Supp. 1328 (W.D.N.Y. 1979).

12. *Stuart*, 443 F. Supp. at 1241.

13. *Id.*

14. 20 U.S.C. §1415(b)(1)(C); 34 C.F.R. §300.504(a); 34 C.F.R. §104.36. *See also, e.g., S-1, supra*, (5th Cir. opinion); *Maher, supra.*

15. 484 U.S. 305, 108 S.Ct.592 (1988).

16. *See e.g., Maher, supra; S-1, supra* (5th Cir. opinion); *Kaelin, supra*; Lamont X. v. Quisenberry, 606 F. Supp. 809 (S.D. Ohio 1984); *Koger, supra; Sherry, supra; Stuart*, 443 F. Supp. at 1242-43.

17. *Maher, supra*; Board of Education v. Illinois State Board of Education, 531 F. Supp. 148 (C.D. Ill. 1982); *Sherry, supra; Stuart, supra.*

18. Brookline School Committee v. Golden, 628 F. Supp. 113, 116 (D. Mass. 1986), *citing* Concerned Parents & Citizens v. New York City Board of Education, 629 F.2d 751 (2d Cir. 1980), *cert. denied*, 449 U.S. 1078 (1981) (school closing not a change in educational placement where children are transferred to similar programs in other schools); *Lamont X., supra* (removal of pupil from classroom to provide homebound tutoring is a change in educational placement); Stock v. Massachusetts Hospital School, 392 Mass. 205, 467 N.E.2d 448 (1984) (the decision to graduate a child, thus terminating his eligibility for special educational services, is a change in educational placement); *S-1, supra* (5th Cir. opinion) (transfer of child from classroom to homebased tutoring is a change in educational placement).

19. 108 S.Ct. at 605 n.8, citing letter from Thomas Bellamy, Director, OSEP to Martha J. Fields, Md. Dept. Educ., 2/26/87, EHLR 211:437.

20. *Id.*

21. 34 C.F.R. §300.505(a).

22. 20 U.S.C. §1415(b)(1)(D); 34 C.F.R. §300.505(b).

23. 34 C.F.R.§104.36; *see also* 34 C.F.R.§104.35(a).

24. *See S-1*, 635 F.2d at 347 (placement decisions under IDEA [EHA] must be made by group knowledgeable about child, meaning of evaluation data, and available options).

25. *S-1*, 635 F.2d at 347; *Stuart*, 443 F. Supp. at 1243, citing 34 C.F.R. §§300.533(a)(3), 300.345.

26. 34 C.F.R. §300.534.

27. 34 C.F.R. §104.35(a).

28. 20 U.S.C. §1415(b)(1)(E); 34 C.F.R.§300.506(a); 34 C.F.R. §104.36.

29. 20 U.S.C. §1415(b)(2); 34 C.F.R. §300.506(a); 34 C.F.R. §104.36.

30. 20 U.S.C. §§1412(5)(B), 1414(a)(1)(C)(iv); 34 C.F.R. §§300.132, 300.227, 300.550 -.553; 34 C.F.R. §§104.4(b)(1)(iv), (3),(5), 104.34(a),(b).

31. 20 U.S.C. §1412(5)(B).

32. *See, e.g., Stuart*, 443 F.Supp. at 1240, 1242-43; *Howard S.*, 454 F. Supp. at 642; Blue v. New Haven Board of Education, 3 EHLR [1980-81 EHLR DEC] 552:401 (D. Conn. 1981). *See also* P-1 v. Shedd, C.A. No.H-78-58, D. Conn. (Consent Decree, March 23, 1979), 1979-80 EHLR DEC 551:164,

modified in part September 16, 1980, 3 EHLR [1980-81 EHLR DEC]
552:236; Mattie T. v. Holladay, CA No.DC-75-31-S, N.D.Miss. (Consent
Decree, January 26, 1979), 1979-80 EHLR DEC 551:109. *Cf.* Southeast
Warren Community School District v. Department of Public Instruction, 285
N.W.2d 173 (Sup. Ct. Iowa 1979) (LEA authorized by state statute to expel
handicapped student provided certain procedures are followed prior to
expulsion, including reevaluation of student by diagnostic team, report and
recommendation of team to school board, and following full hearing by
school board, a determination as to whether an alternative placement will
meet needs of student; expulsion is last resort when no reasonable
alternative placement is available).

33. *Stuart*, 443 F. Supp. at 1240. *See also S-1*, 635 F.2d at 348; *Blue, supra.*

34. *Stuart*, 443 F. Supp. at 1242-43

35. *Maher, supra*; *S-1, supra* (5th Cir. opinion); *Kaelin, supra*; *Lamont X.,
supra*; *Koger, supra*; *Sherry, supra*; *Stuart*, 443 F. Supp. at 1242-43.

36. 484 U.S. at 311, 108 S.Ct. at 597-598.

37. 34 C.F.R.§§300.551(b). *See, e.g.*, T.G. v. Board of Education of
Piscataway, N.J., 576 F. Supp. 420 (D.N.J. 1983), *aff'd* 738 F.2d 420 (3rd
Cir. 1984), *cert. denied*, 869 U.S. 1086, 105 S.Ct. 592 (1984).

38. 34 C.F.R. §300.552, concerning the least restrictive placement under
IDEA, quoting the Dept. of Education's analysis of its §504 regulations, 34
C.F.R. Part 104, App. A, para. 24 (regarding 34 C.F.R. §104.34).

39. 20 U.S.C. §1415(e)(3) (emphasis added).

40. 20 U.S.C. §1415(b)(1)

41. 20 U.S.C. §1415(b)(1)(E)

42. 20 U.S.C. §1415(b)(2).

43. 34 C.F.R. §300.513.

44. 20 U.S.C. §1412(2)(B).

45. 20 U.S.C. §1414(a)(1)(A); 34 C.F. R. §300.220.

46. *See* 34 C.F.R. §104.32.

47. *See* Rodriguez v. Bd. of Ed. of Cato-Meridian Central School District,
C.A. No.80-CV-100T (N.D.N.Y., Dec.18,1980)(temporary restraining order
issued prohibiting school system from excluding epileptic plaintiff not
referred or classified from current placement); Doe v. Rockingham School
Board, 658 F. Supp. 403, 410 (W.Va. 1987); In re: Harlingen Consolidated
Indep. School Dist., 3 EHLR [1981-82 EHLR DEC] 503:344 (Texas
Education Agency 1982); *but see* Mrs. A.J. v. Special School Dist. No.1, 478
F. Supp. 418 (D. Minn. 1979)(15 day suspension with evaluation pending).

48. 20 U.S.C. §1415(b)(2); 34 C.F.R. §300.506(a); 34 C.F.R.§104.36.

49. 20 U.S.C. §1415(e)(3); 34 C.F.R. §300.513; *Howard S.*, 454 F. Supp. at
642; *Stuart*, 443 F. Supp. at 1241-42; *Blue, supra*; *cf. Mrs. A.J.*, 478 F. Supp.
at 432 n.13 (neither parental objection to change in placement required by
state law nor a complaint under §1415 to challenge suspension filed).

50. Numerous courts had previously held that disabled children could not be expelled or suspended indefinitely from their current educational placement during the pendency of an administrative or judicial proceeding . See *Kaelin, supra* (expulsion of child during pendency of placement hearings was repugnant to the stay-put provision); *Maher, supra* (disabled youth may not be indefinitely suspended for conduct that is a manifestation of disabling condition during pendency of hearings); *S-1, supra; Koger, supra* (expulsion violated stay-put rights of students whose behaviors were caused by disabling conditions); *Stuart, supra* (expulsion constituted change in educational placement).

51. The Supreme Court did not address the issue of nexus in *Honig* because the individual claimants were in fact emotionally disturbed youth who had been unilaterally subjected to indefinite suspensions on the basis of dangerous and disruptive behavior. Arguably, when a student, who is classified as disabled or who has been referred for evaluation, challenges her suspension or disciplinary sanction on the basis of her statutory entitlements, it should not be necessary for her to demonstrate or prove a nexus between the conduct for which she is being punished and her disability. See discussion, *infra*.

52. 108 S.Ct. at 604.

53. 108 S.Ct. at 596-97, 604.

54. 108 S.Ct. at 604.

55. See comment to 34 C.F.R. §300.513. An emergency situation indicates that issues of health, safety, or substantial disruption are involved, *i.e.*, a child is dangerous to himself or others, or his/her behavior is ongoing and so disruptive that it is significantly impairing the education of other children in the classroom. In this limited instance, school officials are not precluded from suspending a student, *id.*, but not for more than 10 school days in an academic year. Moreover, for an emergency suspension to be warranted, all less restrictive alternatives for dealing with the handicapped child must have been considered, tried, or rejected as inappropriate. *See* 34 C.F.R. §300.505. To comply with the least restrictive environment requirements, an emergency exclusion must be the last resort for eliminating the substantial disruption or the danger to health or safety.

56. 108 S. Ct. at 605.

57. 20 U.S.C. §1415(e)(2).

58. 108 S. Ct. at 606.

59. *Compare* Cronin v. Board of Education of the East Ramapo Central School District, 689 F. Supp. 197, 204-05 (S.D.N.Y. 1988); Abney by Kantor v. District of Columbia Board of Ed., 849 F.2d 1491 (D.C.Cir. 1988); *and* Christopher P. v. Marcus, 915 F.2d 794 (2d Cir. 1990) *with, e.g.*, Board of Education of Township High School District No. 211 v. Corral, 1988-89 EHLR DEC. 441:390 (N.D. Ill. 1989); Board of Ed. of Township High School District No. 211 v. Kurtz-Imig, 16 EHLR 17, (N.D. Ill. 1989); *and* Texas City

Independent School Distr. v. Jorstad, 752 F. Supp. 231 (S.D. Tx. 1990).

60. *Honig*, 108 S.Ct. at 606.

61. *See e.g., Corral, supra; Kurtz-Imig, supra; Jorstad, supra.*

62. *See e.g.,* Stellato v. Board of Education of the Ellenville Central School District, No. 89-CV-749 (N.D.N.Y., Aug. 4, 1989).

63. *See e.g., Lamont X.,* 606 F. Supp. at 815.

64. *See e.g.,* Concerned Parents & Citizens v. New York City Board of Education, 629 F.2d 751 (2d Cir. 1980), *cert. denied,* 449 U.S. 1078 (1981).

65. *See* Inquiry of Baugh, EHLR 211:481 (OSEP 8/12/87).

66. *See also Rockingham County School Board,* 658 F. Supp. at 408.

67. *S-1,* 635 F.2d at 348.

68. *See* Inquiry of New, EHLR 213:258 (OSEP 9/15/89) (stating that §1412(2) requires educational services to be provided to all disabled students during periods of long-term exclusion resulting from non-disability related behavior); Inquiry of Davis, 16 EHLR 734 (OSEP 12/22/89) (stating that OSERS [Office of Special Education and Rehabilitation Services] position that special education students may not be denied education services upon suspension or expulsion applies to all states). *N.B.,* subsequently a federal district court has granted a motion for summary judgment on behalf of a local school district, representing a certified class of all school districts in Indiana, ruling that the Assistant Secretary of OSERS in rendering such interpretation through a letter of policy which was not published in the Federal Register or the Code of Federal Regulations and without complying with the Administrative Procedures Act ("APA"), 5 U.S.C. §553, acted *ultra vires.* See Metropolitan School District of Wayne Township v.Davila, No. IP 90-1435-C, S.D.Ind., Summary Judgment, 8/13/91. In finding the letter written in response to *Inquiry of New* to be a "legislative rule", requiring notice and comment under the APA, not merely an "interpretive rule" exempt from the APA's requirements, the court found that the effect of the "New letter" was "to change a long standing policy of OSERS without a corresponding change in the underlying statute or regulations." *Id.,* slip op. at 13. For a discussion of the extent to which, contrary to the court's ruling, current law supports the right to continued education during any period of lawful exclusion, see Chapter VIII(B)(3), below, concerning the Supreme Court's straightforward interpretation of the plain language of §1415(e)(3) and application to §1412.

69. See discussion *supra,* Chapter VIII(A)(1) through (4); 20 U.S.C. §§1412(2), 1412(5)B), 1415(b)(1)(C), 1415(e)(3); 29 U.S.C. §794, 34 C.F.R. §§104.4(b); Fourteenth Amendment, U.S. Const.

70. *See Stuart, supra; Howard S., supra. But see, S-1,* 635 F.2d at 348-349; *Koger,* 480 F.2d at 229 ("Before a disruptive handicapped child can be expelled, it must be determined whether the handicap is the cause of the child's propensity to disrupt. . .and this issue must be determined through the change in placement procedures required by the [IDEA].")

71. 29 U.S.C.§794; 34 C.F.R. §104.4(b).

72. As the U.S. Supreme Court recognized in *Goss, supra*, to constitute an emergency which would warrant the denial of procedural rights prior to a pupil's removal from school, the pupil's presence must pose a *continuing danger* to persons or property or an *ongoing threat* of conduct which will *actually and substantially interfere* with the ability of other students to learn. *Id.*, 419 U.S. at 582-83. *Cf. Lamont X.* 606 F. Supp. at 816 (defendants did not follow "normal procedure" in responding to arguably "emergency" situation necessitating removal of two pupils with severe behavioral disabilities by imposing long-term change in placement instead of short-term suspension; nor did "a sufficient emergency *persist* to justify exclusion of plaintiffs...") (emphasis added).

73. 29 U.S.C. §794; 34 C.F.R. §104.3(j).

74. 34 C.F.R. §104.33(a); *see* Hairston v. Drosick, 423 F. Supp. 180, 184 (S.D. W.Va. 1976).

75. 34 C.F.R. §104.33(b).

76. 34 C.F.R. §104.35.

77. See 34 C.F.R. §104.4(b).

78. *See* Seattle (WA) School District No. 1, EHLR 257:203 (OCR 10/16/80); Inquiry of Rhys, EHLR 254:26 (OCR 4/15/85); Inquiry of Smith, OCR, EHLR 305:51 (OCR 4/24/89) (reflecting change in OCR definition of "significant change in placement" as exclusion for more than 10 consecutive school days, rather than 10 cumulative school days per school year; recognizing that shorter suspensions may constitute a change in placement if they create a pattern of exclusion); *see also*, Memorandum to OCR Senior Staff from William L. Smith, Acting Assistant Secretary for Civil Rights, re: "Suspension of handicapped students - deciding whether misbehavior is caused by a child's handicapping condition," 11/13/89, 16 EHLR 491 (disabled student may not be removed for more than 10 days without a "manifestation determination" based on recent, relevant information, including psychological data related to the student's behavior, by a group of persons knowledgeable about the student and special education).

79. Courts have recognized without distinguishing between §504 and IDEA that a school's "handling of the plaintiff may have contributed to her disruptive behavior," *Stuart*, 443 F. Supp. at 1241; that an inappropriate educational placement can cause anti-social behavior, Frederick L. v. Thomas, 408 F. Supp. 832, 825 (E.D. Pa. 1976); that "expulsion of a handicapped child may not be considered until it has been established that the disruptive behavior is not the result of an inappropriate placement," *Koger*, 480 F. Supp. at 229; that the school district made "no effort" to determine whether plaintiff's incidents of misconduct were related to his disability," *Howard S.*, 454 F. Supp. at 635; and found that plaintiff, whom school officials sought to expel following a suicide attempt and hospitalization, "was not afforded free, appropriate public education during

the period from the time he enrolled in high school until December of 1976,[which] was,. . . a contributing and proximate cause of his emotional difficulties and emotional disturbance." *Id.*, 454 F. Supp. at 640. *Cf.* Chris D. v. Montgomery County Board of Education, 753 F. Supp. 922 (M.D. Ala. 1990) (school failed to provide appropriate educational program to emotionally disturbed student where, rather than employing strategies to teach him appropriate behavior with the goal of ultimately returning to the regular education setting, IEP merely described classroom rules and punishments and rewards for breaking or following them; student had repeatedly been subject to disciplinary sanctions).

80. *See e.g.*, St. Ann v. Palisi, 495 F.2d 423 (5th Cir. 1974) (in the absence of personal guilt, non-disabled children's substantive due process rights violated by suspension and later transfer to another school as a result of mother's having struck assistant principal); *see also Howard S.*, 454 F. Supp. at 638; *Hairston*, 423 F. Supp. at 182-83 (disabled child's right to education could not be conditioned on her mother's presence at school); *Sherry*, 479 F. Supp. at 1339 (indefinite suspension of student with severe disabilities was unlawful and cannot be justified by defendants' concern for her safety; such concern could have been eliminated had defendants provided the necessary supervision as part of plaintiff's appropriate education program); Teresa Diana P. v. Alief Independent School District, 744 F.2d 484 (5th Cir. 1984) (maintenance of action for attorney fees rested on constitutional claims independent of EHA where right of child with disabilities to attend school was conditioned on mother's compulsory attendance in group psychotherapy sessions).

81. See 34 C.F.R. §300.5(b)(8)(ii)).

82. *See* 20 U.S.C. §§1412(2)(C), 1414(1)(A); 34 C.F.R. §§300.128, 300.200; 34 C.F.R. 104.32. *See also* Frederick L. v. Thomas, 557 F.2d 373 (3rd Cir.1977) (court order requiring school district to submit plan for identification of handicapped students under state law); Panitch v. Wisconsin, 444 F. Supp. 320 (E.D. Wis. 1977)(state's failure to insure that handicapped children were identified and provided special education violated equal protection); Mattie T. v. Holladay, No. DC-75-31-S (N.D. Miss., July 29, 1977)(absence of an adequate plan to locate and identify handicapped children throughout the state, in violation of IDEA [then the EHA]).

83. 20 U.S.C. §§1412(a)(C), 1414(a)(1)(A); 34 C.F.R. §§300.128(a)(1), 300.220; 34 C.F.R. §104.35.

84. *See* Rodriguez v. Board of Education of the Cato-Meridien Central School District, C.A.No.80-CV-100T (N.D.N.Y.)(TRO 12/18/80); *Rockingham School Board*, 658 F. Supp. at 410.

85. C.A. No. 80-CV-100T (N.D.N.Y.) (TRO 12/18/80). For another helpful case on the rights of students not yet classified or referred, see *Rockingham School Board*, 658 F. Supp. at 410.

86. *See* 29 U.S.C. §706, as amended by §111(a) of the Rehabilitation Act Amendments of 1974; 34 C.F.R. §§104.3(j)(1), (j)(2)(i)-(iv); also see discussion in Chapter I, *supra*, concerning the broad definition for eligibility under §504, and analogous argument for inclusion in cases cited in Chapter VII, *supra*, concerning students with AIDS or who test HIV positive.

87. *See e.g.*, Cook v. Edwards, 341 F. Supp. 307 (D.N.H. 1972).

88. *See, e.g.*, Garcia v. Miera, 817 F.2d 650, 652-56 (10th Cir. 1987), *cert. denied*, 108 S.Ct. 1220 (1988)("grossly excessive corporal punishment").

89. 34 C.F.R. §104.3(j)(2)(iv).

90. 34 C.F.R. §104.3(j)(2)(iii).

91. 34 C.F.R. §300.5(b)(8)(ii).

92. 34 C.F.R. §104.4(b), 34 C.F.R. §104.33-37.

93. 34 C.F.R. part 104, App. A, para. 4.

94. 34 C.F.R.§104.33(b).

95. 29 U.S.C.§706(8).

96. 29 U.S.C. §706(8)(C)(ii).

97. 29 U.S.C.§706(8)(C)(iv), as amended.

98. 34 C.F.R.§104.35(b).

99. 34 C.F.R.§104.36.

100. *See Goss, supra.*

101. *See Stuart, supra; Howard S., supra. But see S-1,* 635 F.2d at 348-349; *Koger,* 480 F.2d at 229 ("Before a disruptive handicapped child can be expelled, it must be determined whether the handicap is the cause of the child's propensity to disrupt. . .and this issue must be determined through the change in placement procedures required by the Handicapped Act.")

102. 108 S.Ct. at 604, 605.

103. 108 S. Ct. at 596-7, 604-05.

104. *Id.*

105. *Compare* School Board of the County of Prince William v. Malone, 762 F.2d 1210 (4th Cir. 1985) (upholding nexus between conduct of acting as conduit in three drug transactions in which plaintiff had taken no drugs nor profited financially and his learning disability, which prevented his comprehending or giving long-term consideration to the consequences of his actions) *with Maher,* 793 F.2d at 1480 n.8 (distinguishing "conduct that bears only an attenuated relationship to the child's handicap", i.e., where a child's physical handicap results in his loss of self esteem, and the child consciously misbehaves to gain attention, or win approval of his peers from conduct that is "caused by" the handicap which "significantly impairs the child's behavioral control").

106. See discussion in §VIII(B)(3), below, and cases cited therein.

107. *See e.g.*, Green v. Johnson, 513 F. Supp. 965 (D. Mass. 1981); Milonas v. Williams, 691 F.2d 931 (10th Cir. 1982), *cert. denied* 460 U.S. 1069, 103 S.Ct. 1524.

108. *See e.g.*, Christopher P. v. Marcus, 915 F.2d 794 (2d Cir. 1990).

109. See, e.g., Flint Board of Education v. Williams, 88 Mich. App. 8, 276 N.W.2d 499 (1979)(probate court has no jurisdiction over school petition based on violation of school rules and regulations when parent has requested an administrative hearing); In the Interest of J.G., Case No. 88-JC-149, Dist. Ct., Shawnee Cty., KA, Journal entry, 11/28/89 (judgment upheld ordering "child in need of care" be placed in educational setting determined by school district despite objection under IDEA of parent whose educational rights had not been terminated); In the Matter of Shelly Maynard, 453 N.Y.S.2d 352 (Family Ct., Monroe Cty. 1982)(where juvenile's disability was identified only after court involvement, school must follow obligations under state education law; court should become involved only if disabled child fails to attend appropriate educational placement); In the Interest of J.D., 510 So.2d 623 (Fla. App. 1 Dist. 1987)(court did not have jurisdiction over minor child allegedly in need of placement in educable mentally disabled classroom placement; educational needs of child did not form statutory basis of dependency); In re Tony McCann, C.A. No. 158, 17 EHLR 551 (Ct. App. Tenn. 2/27/90)(reversing finding of "unruly child" based on juvenile court's statutorily limited jurisdiction; school district's filing of "unruly" petition changed child's educational placement, violated his rights under IDEA and state law, and failed to follow mandated administrative procedures).

110. See, e.g., Matter of P.J., 575 N.E.2d 22 (Ind. App. 3 Dist. 1991) (upholding juvenile court's issuance of injunction forbidding public school district from expelling a Child In Need of Services for drinking alcohol on school property in light of irreparable harm if youth not permitted to return to school following disclosure of sexual molestation; note also the dissent's reference to "this inappropriate extension of the judiciary's role into the province of school officials"); *In the Matter of Shelly Maynard, supra.*

111. *In re: Tony McCann, supra.*

112. *Id.*, 17 EHLR at 553, slip op. at 8, citing *In the Matter of Shelly M., supra.*

113. 635 F.2d 342 (5th Cir. 1981).

114. *S-1*, 635 F.2d at 348.

115. *Kaelin, supra. See also Lamont X., supra; Rockingham County School Board, supra.*

116. 793 F.2d 1470 (9th Cir. 1986).

117. *Maher*, 793 F.2d at 1482, footnote omitted.

118. *Id.*

119. See discussion at note 10, *supra*, and cases cited therein. Also see note 66, *supra*.

IX.
Early Intervention Services for Infants and Toddlers

In 1986 Congress enacted P.L.99-457[1], which amended IDEA to create a discretionary early intervention program for eligible infants and toddlers (birth through age 2) and their families.[2] Authorizing federal financial assistance to states willing to develop and implement this comprehensive, inter-agency program, Congress acknowledged the link between early child development and learning and specifically sought to enhance the development of infants and toddlers manifesting developmental delay, to minimize the likelihood for potential delay among children seriously "at risk", and to enhance the capacity of families to meet their children's special needs.[3]

Each of the fifty states which have elected to participate in this grant-in-aid program is required to select a lead state agency to coordinate all available state resources and resolve interagency disputes regarding the provision of early intervention services.[4] Federal dollars received during the first three years of participation have been used primarily for planning; they may also be used for direct services not covered by other sources to expand or enhance services, but may not be utilized to replace existing funding or to reduce benefits or assistance to eligible children.

The law requires that services be provided at no cost. However, federal or pre-existing state laws may authorize fees for certain services.[5] In this instance a state may charge on a sliding scale,[6] but cannot deny services to eligible infants and toddlers whose families are unable to pay the fee.[7]

The statute, as amended, defines "infants and toddlers with disabilities" as children from birth through age two who need early intervention services because they are experiencing developmental delays in one or more areas of cognitive development, physical development, language and speech development, psychosocial development, or self-help skills, or have a diagnosed physical or mental condition that has a good chance of resulting in developmental delay.[8] Significantly, the term may also include, at a state's discretion, "individuals from birth to age two, inclusive," who are "at risk" of having substantial developmental delays if early intervention services are not provided."[9] The statute allows each state to adopt its own definitions of "developmental delay" and "at risk."[10] In developing definitions for "at risk" children, states are free to include biological factors identified during the neonatal period (*e.g.* low birth weight, respiratory distress) and/or environmental factors.[11]

A. Quality and Individualization

A unique aspect of this federal law is its focus on the family rather than the child in isolation. The legislation requires that a child's needs be assessed in the context of his/her family's strengths and needs.[12] In addition, participating states are required to provide early intervention services to each eligible infant or toddler and his or her family in conformity with a written, individualized, family service plan (IFSP).[13] The IFSP is intended to assist parents in meeting their child's special needs, to provide on-going support to parents, and to involve parents as active participants in their child's development.[14] The federal law and its implementing regulations recognize that the optimal outcome of this family-focused program is for parents to learn about their child's needs, and how they, as caretakers, can enhance their infant or toddler's development.[15]

The IFSP must include "a statement of the major outcomes expected to be achieved for the infant or toddler and the family, and the criteria, procedures, and timelines used" for determining the degree to which progress toward achieving the outcomes is being made.[16] In addition, the plan must identify the specific early intervention services necessary to meet the needs of the infant or toddler and family, including the frequency, intensity, and method of delivering services, the anticipated duration of such services, the case manager responsible for coordinating the delivery of services and implementing the plan, and steps to be taken to support the transition of the toddler to special education services under Part B of IDEA if such services are appropriate.[17] The IFSP must be reviewed at least every six months to determine the degree to which progress toward achieving the identified outcomes is being made and to make any modifications or revisions in outcomes and services.[18]

The plan is jointly developed by the family and qualified personnel involved in the provision of services to the child. It is based on a multidisciplinary evaluation and assessment of the child and an assessment of the child's family.[19] However, because of the relative rapidity of infant development, actual intervention services may commence with the parents' consent prior to completion of the family plan.[20] Early intervention services designed to meet the individual needs of eligible infants and toddlers and their families may include, *but are not limited to*, family training; counseling and home visits; special instruction; speech pathology and audiology; occupational therapy; physical therapy; psychological services; case management services; medical services for diagnostic or evaluation purposes; early identification, screening, and assessment services; and health services "necessary to enable the infant or toddler to benefit from the other early intervention services."[21] Vision services, assistive technology devices and assistive technology services, and transportation would be included under this non-inclusive definition of early intervention services. Furthermore, these services must be provided by qualified persons, including special educators, psychologists, nutritionists, physicians, nurses, physical and occupational therapists, and social workers.[22]

B. Parent Participation, Accountability and Enforcement

Having learned from the model developed by the Head Start program, Congress included parents as critical players in the early intervention system. Without parental consent, children in need of early intervention services will remain unserved; and as evidenced by research findings, without ongoing parent support and involvement, the impact of early intervention services will be limited. The statute and its implementing regulations underscore Congress' intent to promote collaborative decision-making among parents and professionals and to prevent coerced participation in programs.

Parents' written consent must be obtained before conducting an initial evaluation and assessment of a child or family and prior to initiating early intervention services and/or changing the services provided a child or family.[23] The parent must be fully informed of all information relevant to the activity for which consent is sought in his/her native language or other mode of communication, agree in writing, and understand that consent is voluntary and revocable at any time.[24] To address, and it is hoped, to overcome the fear, distrust and suspicion of many parents, states are affirmatively obliged under the Act to pursue activities designed to encourage parental consent to recommended evaluation and assessment procedures and to early intervention services.[25] Such activities might include providing parents with relevant information or offering peer counselling to enhance their understanding of the value of early intervention and to allay concerns about their participation in the state's program.

Consistent with the research in parent involvement, the statute manifests its commitment to utilize the skills of parents through the inclusion of "parent to parent" support personnel as possible "qualified" persons who could offer early intervention services.[26] For example, "parent to parent" support personnel might be particularly effective in providing "family training, counseling and home visits." A parent who has already participated in the early intervention process with his/her child could be an exceptional source of information and support for less experienced parents. Furthermore, using "parent support personnel" in early intervention programs is one way that states might attract employees who are more representative of the communities and cultures of those children and families receiving services.

Part H of Public Law 99-457 creates a federal statutory entitlement to early intervention services for eligible infants, toddlers, and their families residing in participating states. The Act provides a five year phase-in-period for states to plan, develop, and implement a statewide, comprehensive, coordinated system of early intervention services. Acceptance of fourth year funding obligates states to implement the assurances contained in their fourth year applications, including, that evaluations and assessments are conducted, an IFSP is developed for each child determined to be eligible and the child's family, and case management services are available to each eligible child and the child's family.[27] States are also required by their fourth year application to adopt and implement procedural safeguards consistent with the federal statute.[28]

In addition to substantial protection concerning notice and informed consent, the new statute mandates, among other things, that parents have a right to have an administrative complaint timely resolved, including through a due process hearing before an independent decisionmaker, and the right to file a civil action in state or federal court.[29] In its fifth year application,[30] each participating state must assure that prior to beginning its fifth year of participation, an IFSP will be developed and implemented for each eligible infant and toddler and the child's family. Thus, upon receipt of funding based on fifth year applications, states must have appropriate early intervention services available to all eligible infants and toddlers and their families.[31]

[NOTE: This section was excerpted in large part from Boundy, *Changing Educational Outcomes for Young Children from Low-Income Families*, 24 Clearinghouse Review 375 (Special Issue, 1991)].

Notes

1. 100 Stat. 1145 (1986), Education of the Handicapped Act Amendments of 1986, codified at 20 U.S.C. §§1462-1485.

2. P.L. 99-457 also strengthened the incentive for all states to serve those three to five year old children with disabilities not already being provided with special educational services. See discussion in Chapter I, *supra*.

3. See 20 U.S.C. §1471(a).

4. 20 U.S.C. §1476(b)(9).

5. 20 U.S.C. §1472(2)(B); 34 C.F.R. §§303.12(a)(3)(iv), 303.521(a).

6. *Id.*

7. 34 C.F.R. §303.520(3)(ii). The regulations also identify specific functions that must be done by the state at no cost to parents, including child find, evaluation and assessment, case management, development, review and evaluation of individualized family service plans (IFSPs), and implementation of procedural safeguards. See 34 C.F.R. §303.521(b).

8. 20 U.S.C. §1472(1).

9. *Id.*

10. 34 C.F.R. §§303.160, 303.300.

11. To date, at least one third of participating states have chosen to extend eligibility to "at risk" children. For the reasons explained *infra* at note 30, however, it is premature to assume that these states will actually serve at-risk children when the entitlement provisions of P.L. 99-457 take effect.

12. 20 U.S.C. §§1476(b)(3), 1477(a)(1).

13. 20 U.S.C. §1472(2)(G), 1477(a)(2).

14. 20 U.S.C. §§1471(a)(4), 1477(d), 1480(3).

15. *See, e.g.*, 20 U.S.C. §1477(d)(2); 34 C.F.R. §303.322(d)(1).

16. 20 U.S.C. §1477(d)(3).

17. 20 U.S.C. §1477(d)(4)-(7).

18. 20 U.S.C. §1477(b); 34 C.F.R. §303.342(b).

19. 20 U.S.C. §1477(a).

20. 20 U.S.C. §1477(c).

21. 20 U.S.C. §1472(2)(E).

22. 20 U.S.C. §1472(2)(F).

23. 20 U.S.C. §§1477(c), 1480(5), (6); 34 C.F.R. §§303.322(d)(2), 303.403, 303.404(a)(1), 303.404(a)(2).

24. 20 U.S.C. §1480(5); 34 C.F.R. §§303.401, 303.403.

25. 20 U.S.C. §1476(6).

26. 20 U.S.C. §1476(b)(8); Note 2 to 34 C.F.R. §303.12.

27. 34 C.F.R. §303.150, 34 C.F.R.§§303.160-303.175.

28. 20 U.S.C. §§1476(b)(12), 1480.

29. See 20 U.S.C. §1480.

30. Because of the complexity and costs associated with providing mandatory early intervention services to all eligible infants and toddlers by the fifth year of a state's participation under Part H, economic recession, and limited federal funding, many states (reportedly 15-20) were considering dropping out of the discretionary program. Therefore, Congress, involved in the reauthorization of Part H of IDEA, enacted H.R. 2127 in May, 1991 as a specific emergency amendment to another bill (extending the Rehabilitation Act), to allow states that were not prepared to meet the *fourth year* requirements of Part H one additional year of planning time before being required to meet the requirements of year *four*. This bill allows those States that are behind schedule and not prepared to meet all the fourth year requirements in FY 1990 and all fifth year requirements in FY 1991 to request "extended participation". Each state is limited to two one-year requests for extended participation. Thereafter, they must meet all *fifth* year requirements to be eligible for further funding. The bill was signed by the President in early June, 1991.

Under a differential funding formula, states that repeat their third year planning will be funded at the same level as the prior year, and the incremental dollars they would otherwise have received for fourth year participation will be proportionately distributed to those states that have had their fourth year applications approved and that remain on the five-year schedule.

31. 34 C.F.R. §303.152, §303.302; *see also* Office for Special Education Programs, U.S. Dept. of Education, Response of Judy A. Schrag, Director, to inquiry [dated 4/2/91] of Rita Schmidt, Dept. of Health and Social Services, Alaska; 1 Early Childhood Law and Policy Reporter [ECLPR] §65.

Appendix A

Guide To Legal Notations And References Used In This Book

Legal citations (or "cites") such as those found in the endnotes of this book contain the basic information needed to locate court decisions, statutes, regulations, decisions of administrative agencies, journal articles and other information. These volumes can generally be found in law libraries at law schools, state houses, and federal and state courthouses. There is a standardized format and set of abbreviations used in citations, depending on the source of the information.

CITATIONS TO COURT DECISIONS

The bound volumes in which court decisions are published are called "reporters." A typical case citation to a reporter looks like this:

Wood v. Davison, 351 F. Supp. 543 (N.D. Ga. 1972)

In other words, the case in which Wood sued Davison was decided by the United States District Court for the Northern District of Georgia in 1972. The court's opinion can be found in volume 351 of the reporter entitled Federal Supplement, at page 543. Where more than one page number is listed — for example, "351 F. Supp. 543, 545 (N.D. Ga. 1972)" — the first page number (543) indicates where the opinion begins, while the second page number (545) indicates where the specific point being cited can be found. The citation "351 F. Supp. at 545" refers to a point being made at page 545 of the opinion.

The decisions issued by the various levels or types of courts are each published in a separate series of volumes. The following information indicates how to recognize and locate decisions in legal reporters.

U.S. Supreme Court Abbreviations — "U.S." or "S.Ct or "L.Ed."

Decisions of the United States Supreme Court can be found in any one of three published reporters: the United States Reports (U.S.), the Supreme Court Reporter (S.Ct.), or the Lawyer's Edition (L.Ed.).

Example: 394 U.S. 294, 75 S.Ct. 753, 99 L.Ed. 1083 (1955)

In this citation, 394 is the volume number, U.S. indicates United States Reports, and 294 is the page number. The decision was reached in 1955. Supreme Court citations do not contain a court reference next to the date inside the parentheses. Instead, the court is indicated by the reporter abbreviation (U.S. or S.Ct.) alone.

Federal Court of Appeals Abbreviations — "F.2d" and "Cir."

Example: 424 F.2d 1281 (1st Cir. 1970)

A decision by a federal court of appeals, in this case the United States Court of Appeals for the First Circuit, in 1970. This decision can be found in volume 424 of the Federal Reporter, 2nd Series at page 1281.

The courts of appeals are the second highest level in the federal court system, and generally review the decisions of the federal district courts within a specific geographic region. (A map showing which states are included in each federal judicial circuit appears opposite the title page of each volume of West's *Federal Reporter*, 2d series.) (See "Effect and Weight of Court Decisions," below.)

Federal District Court Abbreviations — "F. Supp." and "D."

Example: 300 F. Supp. 748 (N.D. Miss. 1969)

A decision by the federal district court, in this case in the Northern District of Mississippi in 1969. The decisions of these courts are reported in the Federal Supplement, in this case at page 748 of volume 300.

Each state has at least one federal district court. In states which have only one, it is abbreviated as D., such as D.Mass. In addition to North, South, East, or West, a few states also have a Middle District (M.D. Ala.) or a Central District (C.D. Cal.). The district courts are the lowest, or trial court, level in the federal court system.

State Court Abbreviations

 Example: 62 N.J. 473, 303 A.2d 273 (1973)

A state appellate court decision. These decisions can be found in either of two places, the state reporter (here page 473 of volume 62 of the New Jersey Reporter) or the regional reporter which reports the state appellate cases for several states in a region (here the Atlantic Reporter, 2nd Series). Other regions are Pacific (P.), South Western (S.W.), North Western (N.W.), Southern (So.), South Eastern (S.E.), and North Eastern (N.E.). Each of these regional reporters also has a second series for more modern cases.

The particular court will be indicated in the parentheses or can be determined by looking at the reporter abbreviation. Where, as in the case above, no court level is indicated, the decision was issued by the State's supreme court. Examples of lower state court abbreviations are "Ill.App." (Illinois Court of Appeals) and "Pa.Super." (Pennsylvania Superior Court). [In New York State, however, the highest court is actually the Court of Appeals (Ct.App.), while the state Supreme Court (Sup.Ct.) is in fact a lower level court.]

Unreported Cases

If a decision has not been published in a reporter (at least as of the time this book was published), it is cited as in the following example:
 Mattie T. v. Holladay, No. DC-75-31-S (N.D. Miss., July 29, 1977).
The decision can be obtained from the clerk of the court in which the case was decided. (In the above example, it is the U.S. District Court for the Northern District of Mississippi.)

Education for the Handicapped Law Report —"EHLR"

Education for the Handicapped Law Report is a specialized reporter publishing selected decisions in special education cases from both federal and state courts. "EHLR" also publishes selected state due process hearing decisions, decisions of the U.S. Department of Education/Office of Civil Rights ("OCR") on §504 matters, and selected letters and policy statements of the U.S. Department of Education/Office of Special Education Programs ("OSEP") regarding

IDEA requirements. The EHLR format has changed since the reporter first started; EHLR materials are cited here in three ways:

17 EHLR 267 (M.D. Ala. 1990) — A 1990 decision by the federal district court for the Middle District of Alabama, beginning on page 267 of volume 17 of the EHLR.

1986-87 EHLR DEC. 558:143 (2nd Cir. 1986) — A 1986 decision of the U.S. Court of Appeals for the Second Circuit, beginning on page 558:143 of the 1986-87 volume of EHLR decisions.

EHLR 352:185 (OCR 4/18/86) — An Apil 18, 1986 complaint decision or other document by the U.S. Department of Education's Office of Civil Rights, published at page 352:185 of the EHLR volume containing OCR materials for that year. A citation in this format which refers to **"OSEP"** rather than **"OCR"** means a U.S. Department of Education/Office of Special Education Programs letter, policy statement or other document. (See "Effect And Weight Of OCR Decisions And OSEP Policy Letters And Interpretations," below.)

[NOTE: The EHLR has changed its name to Individuals with Disabilities Education Law Report, effective April 5, 1991. Further information may be obtained from the publisher, LRP Publications, Horsham, Pennsylvania.]

CITATIONS TO STATUTES AND REGULATIONS

Federal Statutes — "U.S.C."

Example: 20 U.S.C. §1400 (the first section of the Individuals with Disabilities Education Act)

A "statute" is a law passed by Congress or a state legislature. The statute here is Section 1400 of Title 20 of the United States Code. The United States Code is the permanent system for maintaining federal statutes, and it can be found in bound volumes in law libraries. The words in parentheses refer to the commonly used name of the legislation enacted by Congress.

Federal Regulations — "C.F.R." or "Fed. Reg."

Example: 34 C.F.R. §300.2

Title 34, Section 300.2 of the Code of Federal Regulations, which is the permanent system for maintaining the regulations issued by various federal agencies and departments to implement the statutes passed by Congress. The regulations are legally binding unless and until someone demonstrates to a court that the regulations go beyond what the statute authorizes.

Example: 40 Fed. Reg. 18998 (June 20, 1975)

Page 18998 of volume 40 of the Federal Register. The Federal Register is issued daily and contains newly issued federal regulations when they are proposed, changed, or finally adopted (along with other material issued by federal agencies and departments). Those that are finally adopted are later entered in the Code of Federal Regulations as well (see above).

EFFECT AND WEIGHT OF COURT DECISIONS

Only the decisions of courts which have jurisdiction in a particular geographical area represent the clear judicial interpretation of the law for that area. Thus, for example, schools in Boston are obligated to follow the law as interpreted by the United States Supreme Court, the United States Court of Appeals for the First Circuit, the United States District Court of the District of Massachusetts, and the various relevant state courts. Nevertheless, the decisions of courts in other jurisdictions are relevant in that they will generally be given some weight by courts in your jurisdiction, and they serve as indications of judicial reasoning.

EFFECT AND WEIGHT OF OCR DECISIONS AND OSEP POLICY LETTERS AND INTERPRETATIONS

OCR's regional offices investigate and issue decisions on §504 complaints. OCR has ruled that the decisions of one regional office are binding on other regions. Neither OCR's interpretations of §504 nor OSEP's interpretations of IDEA are binding on courts, although they may be influential. They are binding on states and school systems unless successfully challenged in court.

OTHER NOTATIONS

§   Section
supra   Above
infra   Below
aff'd   Affirmed. The higher court, cited after the abbreviation, has reviewed and upheld the decision of the lower court, cited before the abbreviation.
aff'g   Affirming. The first citation is the higher, reviewing court, and the second is to the lower court decision.
rev'd, rev'g   Reversed, Reversing. On appeal, the higher court has reviewed and reversed the decision of the lower court.
vacated as moot   The order of the lower court has been lifted because by the time the case was appealed, there was no longer a "live" controversy. This might occur, for instance, when a court refuses to order a school to readmit a suspended student, but the student has graduated before the appeal of the court's decision is heard. An order which has been vacated is no longer legally binding, but the opinion may still be cited as evidence of the court's legal reasoning.
vacated on other grounds, reversed on other grounds   The lower court's order is no longer legally binding, but the decision on appeal does not affect the legal reasoning in the portion of the decision which has been cited.
cert. denied   The Supreme Court "denied certiorari" — i.e., it has declined to review the case, and it is expressing no opinion concerning the lower court decision, which remains standing.
Cf.   The case supports a statement, opinion, or conclusion of law different from that in the text but sufficiently analogous to lend some support to the statement in the text.
But see   The case strongly suggests a contrary proposition from the preceding statement in the text.
But cf. The case supports a proposition which, while not directly contradictory to the preceding statement in the text, is sufficiently analogous to suggest a contrary conclusion.

Appendix B

Regional Offices
U.S. Department of Education
Office for Civil Rights

As explained in Chapter VI, individuals (or organizations) who believe that a state or school system is violating §504 may file a complaint with the Office for Civil Rights of the U.S. Department of Education. Complaints should be filed with the appropriate regional office, as follows:

Region I   **(CT, ME, MA, NH, RI, VT)**
U.S. Dept. of Education — Office for Civil Rights
John W. McCormack Post Office and Courthouse
Boston, MA 02109-4557   (617) 223-9667

Region II   **(NJ, NY, Puerto Rico, Virgin Islands)**
U.S. Dept. of Education — Office for Civil Rights
26 Federal Plaza
New York, NY 10278-02-1060   (212) 264-5180

Region III   **(DE, DC, MD, PA, VA, WV)**
U.S. Dept. of Education — Office for Civil Rights
3535 Market Street
Philadelphia, PA 19104-03-2060   (215) 596-6787

Region IV   **(AL, FL, GA, KY, MS, NC, SC, TN)**
U.S. Dept. of Education — Office for Civil Rights
101 Marietta Tower
Atlanta, GA 30323-04-3088   (404) 331-2954

Region V   **(IL, IN, MI, OH, WI)**
U.S. Dept. of Education — Office for Civil Rights
401 S. State Street
Chicago, IL 60605-05-4060   (312) 886-3456

Region VI   **(AR, LA, NM, OK, TX)**
U.S. Dept. of Education — Office for Civil Rights
1200 Main Tower
Dallas, TX 75202-06-5060   (214) 767-3959

Region VII   **(IA, KS, MO, NE)**
U.S. Dept. of Education — Office for Civil Rights
10220 N. Executive Hills Blvd.
P.O. Box 901381
Kansas City, MO 64190-1381-07-6060   (816) 891-8026

Region VIII   **(CO, MT, ND, SD, UT, WY)**
U.S. Dept. of Education — Office for Civil Rights
1961 Stout Street
Denver, CO 80294-08-7060   (303) 844-5695

Region IX   **(AZ, CA, Guam, HI, NV, Trust Terr. of Pacific Is.,**
U.S. Dept. of Education — Office for Civil Rights   **Amer. Samoa)**
221 Main Street
San Francisco, CA 94105-09-8010   (415) 744-3060

Region X   **(AK, ID, OR, WA)**
U.S. Dept. of Education — Office for Civil Rights
915 Second Avenue
Seattle, WA 98174-1099   (205) 442-6811

About The Authors

Eileen L. Ordover, a Staff Attorney at the Center for Law and Education, is a long-time activist and advocate on disability rights issues. As an attorney at the Disabilities Rights Center in Concord, New Hampshire and in private practice in Boston, she represented many children with disabilities and their families.

Kathleen B. Boundy, a recognized authority on special education law, is Co-Director of the Center for Law and Education, where she has represented the rights of children and youth with disabilities for fifteen years. She has participated in major litigation, assisted in drafting critical legislation, and advised attorneys nationwide on educational issues affecting students with disabilities.

Both authors continue to provide training, advice and technical assistance to advocates who represent low-income children with disabilities. In their role as co-counsel with attorneys around the country, they represent the concerns of low-income students with disabilities before state and federal legislative and administrative bodies and in the courts.